LAND OF ISRAEL HAGGADAH

LAND OF ISRAEL

HAGGADAH

Interpreted by
Yona Zilberman

Design & Photos by
Haim Ron

Adama Books

ISBN-0-915361-78-7
MODAN PUBLISHING
Distributors of Adama Books
P.O.Box 1202 • Bellmore, New York 11710
Tel. (516) 679-1380 • Fax: (516) 679-1448

The Land of Israel Hagaddah

Introduction

The Passover hagaddah describes the history of the People of Israel from their very beginnings. Its focal point is the story of the Exodus — the story of the Exodus from slavery to redemption, of the transition from a life of servitude to one of freedom, the story of the People of Israel becoming a nation.

Each year, on the night of the Passover seder, we return once again to recount the story of the Exodus from Egypt, and the story is a prime motif running throughout Jewish history, passed on from generation to generation, from father to son.

The History of the Hagaddah

In the Bible it is written:

Remember this day, when you departed from the land of Egypt, from the house of slavery.... For seven days will you eat matzot.... And on that day you will speak to your son, saying:

It was for this reason that God did so for me when I came out of Egypt.

(Exodus, XIII, 3,6,8.)

The commandment to "recount" the story of the Exodus is quite an ancient commandment. Already during the period of the First Temple, it was the custom to celebrate a Passover evening seder, on the 14th day of the month of Nissan, at twilight. Passover pilgrims to Jerusalem used to offer up their holiday sacrifices in the Temple, and then they would partake of the meat of their Paschal sacrifice within their own family circles and relate the story of the Exodus to their children. Each family head would decide which details to recount, and it was he who determined the length of his story.

However, over the years the need was felt to establish a unified prayer service for the Paschal sacrifice and a set text for the story of the Exodus from Egypt, especially during the Second Temple era, when the daily, Sabbath and holiday prayers were codified.

A first version of the Passover hagaddah can be found in the Mishnah, in the tracate Psachim, Chapter X, Mishnah 4. There the four questions which the son must ask, are related: "....and here the son asks his father. And if the son is ignorant, his father must instruct him: How is this night different from all other nights.... And he must instruct him in accordance with the son's knowledge.

In response to the son's questions, the father recounts the story of the Exodus from Egypt.

In Psachim, the four glasses of wine are mentioned as well:

And he shall take no fewer than four glasses of wine (Chapter X, Mishnah 1)

In remembrance of history, it opens with condemnation and concludes with praise, from: A wandering Aramean was my father (Deuteronomy, XXVI,5) until the entire episode is concluded

(Psachim, Chapter X, Mishnah 4).

The symbols of Passover are mentioned in that same text:
Whoever does not recite these three things on the Passover, does not meet his obligations, and these are: Pesach [the Paschal sacrifice], Matzah and Bitter Herbs.

The Paschal sacrifice — for God passed over ["pasach" in Hebrew] our fathers' houses in Egypt.
Matzah — for our fathers were redeemed from the land of Egypt.
Bitter Herbs — for the Egyptians embittered our fathers' lives in the land of Egypt (Chapter X, Mishnah 5).

The Mishnah also related to the Hallel preyer — the prayer of thanksgiving — which is recited on the seder eve:
Until which point [in the prayer]? The school of Shamai says: until The Mother of the Sons is Happy, while the school of Hillel says, until Flint, to a Water Fountain. (Chapter X, Mishnah 6)

And at which point is the seder concluded? In the Mishnah it is written:
And it is sealed with the redemption. Rabbi Tarphon says: He who redeemed us and redeemed our fathers from Egypt.... Rabbi Akiva says: So may the the Lord our God and the God of our Fathers Take us to Other Holidays and Festivals which will Come upon us in Peace, Joyful in the Establishment of Your City..., and until, Blessed art Thou, O Lord, the Redeemer of Israel. (Ibid).
In our times the hagaddah is a part of the seder eve. Of course, we cannot speak of a single author or "master of the hagaddah." The hagaddah was not compiled in one day, and it is certain that during the time it was being compiled and edited it underwent additions and deletions.
In our times the hagaddah is a collection of biblical verses, rabbinical commentaries, excerpts from Jewish law, prayers and hymns recited on the seder eve, which is the first evening of the Passover holiday.

In the Passover hagaddah the story of the Exodus from Egypt is set out for the reader, as are explanations for the various foods placed on the seder table. During the course of the story, chapters from the Book of Psalms, holiday hymns and prayers of thanksgiving to God for the miracles He performed for the fathers of the nation are interspersed within the Passover hagaddah text. Legends, laws, songs, poems and sayings are included as well.

A standard version of the hagaddah was established by the seventh-century Rabbi Amram Gaon, head of the Sura Yeshivah.

In the 10th century, Rabbi Sa'adia Gaon, also of the Sura Yeshivah, compiled a different standard version, parts of which are included in the hagaddot of the Jews of Yemen, Jerba and Spain. Maimorides, in his book, Mishnah Torah, compiled an additional version of the hagaddah, an attempt to reconcile the two earlier version and a blend of both.

In most Jewish communities Rabbi Amram Gaon's version of the hagaddah is the accepted text. It appears as part of the Vitry Mahzor, compiled by Rabbi Shmuel of the city of Vitry, France, a student of Rashi who lived in the 11th and 12th centuries.

Over the years, additional versions of the hagaddah have been established, for various communities and diasporas, each in accordance with its own customs. Liturgical poems in praise of the holiday were added, as well as various hymns, including light hymns and poems which were introduced in order to heighten the interest of children.

Since it is necessary to recite the hagaddah in a language which everyone understands, each diaspora translated the hagaddah into its own spoken tongue. Thus, translations exist in a large number of languages. In addition, many varied interpretations of the hagaddic text exist. Each generation lent its own unique and contemporaneous personal touch to the diverse interpretations composed upon sections of the hagaddah.

The standard version of the hagaddah grew and expanded to such a degree that it became difficult to delay its reading until after the holiday meal. Therefore, at some time during the Middle Ages, the custom arose to read the major part of the hagaddah — the four questions, the father's response to them and the explanation of the various holiday symbols — before the meal.

Thus, the seder came to be divided into two parts — before and after the meal — and during each part two of the four glasses of wine are drunk.

In order to help with the organization of the seder during the seder eve, the 13th-century Rabbi Shmuel of Provence laid down a series of mnemonic seder symbols:
Kaddesh U-rechatz [kiddush & the washing of hands] Karpas Yachatz [eating a vegetable & dividing the matzah] • Maggid Rachatz [reciting the hagaddah & the washing of hands before the meal] • Motzi Matzah [reciting the blessing on bread & reciting the blessing on matzah] • Maror Korech [eating bitter herbs & wrapping together matzah and bitter herbs] • Shulchan Orech [sitting down to the holiday meal] • Tzafun Barech [retrieving the (hidden) Afikoman & reciting grace after the meal] • Hallel Nirtzah [reciting the prayer of thanksgiving & having the seder accepted by God].

The first section of the hagaddah includes the four questions, the response to them and an explanation of the holiday symbols; the second section begins with the grace after meals and for the most part contains hymns and chapters from the Book of Psalms.

The seder concludes with a number of hymns and liturgical poems and with the call, Next Year in Jerusalem.

Throughout the centuries more than 3000 different editions of the Passover hagaddah have been published, each containing its own unique coloring and illustrations and each maintaining a high level of style and elegance. Jewish artists took great pains to invest of their talents in creating special drawings and illustrations for the various hagaddoth.
Among the most famous hagaddoth which have been published are: the Prague Hagaddah (1326); Venice Hagaddah (1609); Amsterdam Hagaddah (1695); Sarajevo Hagaddah (1898); Darmstadt Hagaddah, Munich; and, in our own generation, the hagaddot of Arthur Szich, Bodko, Steinhardt and others.

The Order – Seder – of the Hagaddah

*Blessing the Wine: The first of four glasses of wine.

*This is the Bread of Penury: A preface of sorts, an introduction to the hagaddah.

*The Four Questions: The asking of questions by one of the children, for the purpose of comprehending the seder symbols.

*We were Slaves: The beginning of the answer which the father provides in response to the questioning child. It opens with a recollection of history: memories of slavery in Egypt and then the Exodus to freedom.

*Various Commentaries: These refer to the fact that it is incumbent upon everyone, even the sages of each generation, to recount the story of the Exodus from Egypt, …and whoever dwells more upon the Exodus from Egypt, so is this praiseworthy.

The sayings of Rabbi Eliezer, Rabbi Yehoshua, Rabbi Elazar ben Azaryah, Rabbi Akiva and Rabbi Tarphon are quoted.

*With reference to Four Sons: Great importance is ascribed to the commandment, And you shall speak to your son. In this section, four different types of sons are exemplified, and the father must explain the Exodus to each type in accordance with that son's understanding and level of comprehension.

*In the Beginning [our Fathers were] Worshippers of Alien Gods: The story of the origins of the People of Israel, from idol worshippers to worshippers of God. This section opens with condemnation and concludes with praise.

*A Wandering Aramean was my Father: Here, biblical verses relating to the historical story are quoted, as well as explantions relating to details of the story.

*The Ten Plagues: These are listed, along with commentaries on the subject by Rabbi Yehuda, Rabbi Yossi Haglili, Rabbi Elazar and Rabbi Akiva.

*The Paschal Sacrifice, Matzah, Bitter Herbs: Sections from the Mishnah – Psachim, Chapter X – are quoted, which explain the central symbols of the holiday of Passover.

*The Prayer of Thanksgiving; Halleluyah: The first section of the Hallel prayer (Psalms, CXIII-CXVIII). This section is also known as the Egyptian Hallel, because of Psalm CXIV, When Israel Departed from the Land of Egypt.

*The Blessing of Redemption: This blessing is mentioned in the Mishnah, Psachim, Chapter X, Mishnah 6.

*Drinking the Second of Four Glasses of Wine:

*The Blessings on the Wine, on the Washing of Hands before the Meal, on the Matzah and on the Bitter Herbs.

*The Passover Meal: When the meal is concluded, the afikoman is eaten.

*Grace after the Meal: The third glass of wine is poured. Grace is recited, as is the blessing on the wine, and the third glass is then drunk.

*The Preface to the Beginning of the Second Part of the Thanksgiving Prayer: The Pour Out Your Wrath prayer, when a special cup of wine is poured out for Elijah the Prophet.

*The Continuation of the Prayer of Thanksgiving: The fourth glass is poured and the second part of the Hallel prayer is recited.

*For His Lovingkindness Endures Forever: The "Great Hallel," Psalm CXXXVI.

*The Soul of Every Living Being and You Will Be Praised By: The Song Blessing, after which the fourth glass of wine is drunk.

*The Concluding Blessing: A shortened grace, recited after eating cereals, drinking wine or eating fruits for which the Land of Israel is renowned.

*The Passover Seder is Terminated: The conclusion.

*Liturgical Poems and Hymns: And So It Was At Midnight; For Him It Is Seemly, For Him It Is Meet; He Is Mighty; Who Knows [Number] One; One Kid.

*It is customary, after having recited the hagaddah, to recite the Song of Songs.

The Patriarchs & the Land of Israel

In the Bible it is Written that God Promised the Land of Israel to the Patriarchs: And God said to Abram, after Lot had left him: Lift up your eyes and look, from the place where you are standing, northward and southward and eastward and westward. For the entire land which you see, will I give to you and to your descendants, forever. And I will make your descendants [as numerous] as the dust of the earth. So, if one is able to enumerate the dust of the earth, so can your descendants be counted.

(Genesis, XIII, 14-16).

God Repeats His Promise of the Land of Israel, to Isaac:

And He appeared to him and He said: Do not go down to Egypt. Dwell in the land of which I shall tell you. Live in this land, and I will be with you and I will bless you, for to you and your descendants will I give all of these lands.

(Genesis, XXVI, 2).

God Promises the Land to Jacob, Too:

And God said to him: I am God Almighty. Be fruitful and multiply; a nation and a community of nations will come from you, and kings shall come forth from your loins. And the land which I gave to Abraham and to Isaac, to you will I give it and to your descendants after you.

(Genesis, XXXV, 11).

The Exodus from Egypt:

And Pharaoh awakened..., and he called for Moses and Aaron by night, and he said: Rise up and go forth from among my people, both you and the People of Israel.... And on that day did the Lord bring the People of Israel out of the land of Egypt, in all their multitudes.

(Exodus. XII, 30-31;51).

The Promise of the Land to Moses:

And Moses went up from the Plains of Moab to Mount Nebo, to the top of the pinnacle which overlooks Jericho. And the Lord showed him all of the land.... And God said to him: This is the land of which I swore to Abraham, to Isaac and to Jacob, saying, I will give it to your descendants.

(Deuteronomy, XXXIV, 1;4)

The Building Up of the Land by Solomon:

And Solomon was the ruler in all of the kingdoms.... And it was in the 480th year after the Exodus of the Children of Israel from the land of Egypt, in the fourth year, in the month of Ziv – i.e., the second month – of King Solomon's reign over Israel, and he built a house for the Lord.

(I Kings V, 1 & VI, 1).

The Destruction of the First Temple and the Exile of the People of Israel:

In the fifth month, on the seventh day of the month, which was the 19th year of King Nebuchadnezzar, king of Babylon, Nebuzaradan, the captain of the bodyguards, a servant of the king of Babylon, came to Jerusalem. And he burned down the house of the Lord and the king's house and all the houses of Jerusalem. He burned down every impressive house.

(II Kings, XXV, 8).

Cyrus' Announcement of the Construction of the Second Temple:

And in the first year of Cyrus, king of Persia..., he put out a proclamation throughout his kingdom and in a letter, saying: Thus says Cyrus, king of Persia: The Lord, the God of heaven, has given me all the kingdoms of the earth, and He has charged me to build Him a house in Jerusalem, which is in Judea. Whoever among you is of His people, may his God be with him, and let him go up to Jerusalem, which is in Judea, to build the house of the Lord, the God of Israel.

(Ezra, I, 1-3).

The War of the Hashmonaim against the Greeks:

And Judah and his brothers spoke to the people, saying: Behold, the enemy is a plague to us, and now let us go up and purify the temple of the Lord.... And there will be great rejoicing among all the people, for God has removed the disgrace of the nations from upon them. And Judah and his brothers and the entire community of Israel went out to celebrate the consecration of the altar on the 25th day of the month of Kislev, for eight days..., with prayers of praise and thanksgiving to God. (Book of the Macabbis, I)

The Destruction of the Second Temple

In the 3828th year, on the ninth day of the month of Ab, Titus captured Jerusalem, and burnt the Temple down and destroyed the Land.

The Balfour Declaration

His Majesty's Government views with favor the establishment of a national homeland for the People of Israel in the Land of Israel and will do all in its power to simplify the attainment of this goal – but subject to the clear and explicit condition that nothing be done that might infringe upon the civil and religious rights of the non-Jewish communities in the Land of Israel, or on the rights and status of the Jews in other lands.

His Majesty's government (2 November 1917)

The Declaration of the Establishment of the State of Israel:

The Jewish nation has risen up in the Land of Israel, where its spiritual, religious and national character was shaped, where it lived a life of sovereign statehood, in which it created a national and universal cultural heritage and bestowed the eternal Book of Books on the entire world. After the nation had been exiled from its land by force, it remained faithful to the land in whichever lands it was scattered and did not cease from prayer and from the hope to return to its land, to renew within it, its national freedom..... On the 29th of November the united national assembly came to a decision dictating the establishment of the State of Israel in the Land of Israel....

Therefore, have we gathered, members of the national assembly, representatives of the Jewish settlement and the Zionist movement, on the day of the termination of the British mandate over the Land of Israel, and by the authority of our natural and historical right and on the basis of the decision of the united national assembly, we hereby declare the establishment of the Jewish State on the Land of Israel – the State of Israel. (Saturday, the fifth day of the month of Iyar, 5708, 14 May 1948).

The Land of Israel Hagaddah

What is unique about this hagaddah?
The hagaddah you are now holding was designed against the background of the landscape and antiquities of the Land of Israel. This hagaddah depicts vistas of the land as they were reflected through the eyes of painters in previous centuries who longed for and loved the Land of Israel, as well as modern-day landscape photographs of the land. All of these are accompanied by the sages' words of love for the land, its vistas and sites. In this way we hope to cultivate our collective historical memory, to bind the past to the present and to forge a link with the future.

Custom and Symbol on the Eve of the Seder
Remembrance of Slavery:

The People of Israel have been particular about retaining the memory of suffering and the memory of redemption throught the centuries. Why so?
The People of Israel believe that one learns from the past, that memory serves to develop a sensitivity to the state of enslavement and is a means to understanding the value of freedom.

Jewish tradition, based as it is on the remembrance of slavery, commanded the free person in Israel to develop a sensitivity toward the stranger and penurious: And the stranger should not be maltreated, and you should not oppress him, for you were strangers in the land of Egypt.

(Exodus, XXII, 21)

Remember that you were a slave and you know what is the soul of a slave; and today you are free, therefore you must make happy the heart of the poor and the soul of those who are miserable, on the day of your rejoicing.

(Midrash Hagadol)

The Drinking of the Four Glasses:

In the Mishnah it is written: And you shall not take fewer than four glasses of wine (Psachim, Chapter X, Mishnah 1). The Talmud too refers to the four glasses, and there it is written: The rabbis said: The four glasses are incumbent upon all — on men, women and children (all of whom were redeemed).

(Psachim, CVIII, B)

There are various explanations of this custom:
In the Jerusalem Talmud (Psachim, Chapter X) it is written:
Rabbi Yochanan said in the name of Rabbi Bnayah:
The four glasses of wine represent the four terms of redemption mentioned in the story of the Exodus from Egypt: And I took you out — Hotzeiti — from the suffering in Egypt; and I saved you — Hitzalti — from their work; and I redeemed you — Ga'alti — with an outstretched arm and with great blows; and I took you — Lakachti — unto Me as a nation.

(Exodus, VI, 6-7).

Rabbi Yehoshua ben Levi said: The four glasses of wine represent Pharaoh's four cups: And Pharaoh's cup was in my hand..., and I pressed them into Pharaoh's cup and placed the cup in Pharaoh's hand.... And you shall place Pharaoh's cup in his hand. (Genesis XL, 11;13)

Rabbi Levi said: They represent the four kingdoms (which enslaved the People of Israel harshly, after their enslavement in Egypt): Babylon, Media, Greece, Edom.

And this is Abarbanel's interpretation, that they represent four redemptions in different historical eras:
The People of Israel were redeemed by means of four sorts of redemption: The first redemption took place when the Holy One, Blessed Be He chose our father Abraham, and of his seed and from him established the People of Israel.

The second redemption was from Egypt.

The third redemption was that the Holy One, Blessed Be He kept us alive during the long years of exile and saved us from all of our enemies, who wished to eradicate the People of Israel.

The fourth redemption is the redemption to come.

And in the book, The Sons of Issascar it is written: It is for this reason that the People of Israel were deemed worthy of the commandment of the four glasses: that they did not change their names; that they did not change their language; that they separated themselves from incest, which they did not commit, and they didn't reveal their secret rites.

It may also be that the drinking of four glasses of wine on the eve of the seder is based, like other customs associated with the order of the festive meal that was practiced during the Second Temple period, on Roman culture. Only free men were permitted to partake of festive meals, and not keeping this decree might have been interpreted as the flagrant violation of a social rule. Drinking four glasses of wine emphasized the transition from slavery to freedom, from enslavement in Egypt to the giving of the Torah.

It is customary to drink red wine. During the periods when the blood libel was rampant, Jews were afraid to use red wine for fear of their neighbors, who claimed that the wine was mixed with the blood of a young Christian boy who had been kidnapped and slaughtered by the Jews. Drinking red wine was an expression of security and freedom from fear.

Eating Matzah

In the first month, on the fourteenth day of the month at evening time, you shall eat matzot....

(Exodus, XII, 18).

One of the central commandments of the Passover holiday is the eating of matzah.
And thus is it written: You shall keep the feast of matzot; seven days will you eat matzot, as I commanded you, at the appointed time in the spring month, for it was at that time that you departed from Egypt.

(Exodus, XXIII, 15).

Eating matzah comes to remind us of the miracle of the Exodus from Egypt.
And in the Passover hagaddah we read: This matzah, what is the reason for it? For there was not enough time for the dough of our fathers to become leavened, before the supreme King of Kings, the Holy One, Blessed Be He, revealed Himself to them and redeemed them.

The matzah symbolizes the bread of penury which our fathers ate when they were slaves in the land of Egypt.

The Three Matzot

Three matzot are placed on the Passover plate, one on top of another. They are designated by the names of three groups of people which constitute the People of Israel.

The uppermost matzah: the Priests [cohen].
The middle matzah: the Levites.
The bottom matzah: the Israelites.

The middle matzah – the Levite – is broken into two unequal parts during the course of the seder. The smaller part remains on the seder plate, while the larger part becomes the afikoman and is hidden. It is customary for the children to steal the afikoman, and towards the end of the seder they are requested to return it. The afikoman is eaten at the close of the meal.

And why are three matzot used?

Two matzot – the top and the bottom – take the place of the two challot which are placed on the Sabbath table, and the Hamotzi blessing is recited over them. The middle matzah signifies the bread of penury which our fathers ate in Egypt. Breaking it in two symbolizes the state of the destitute person, who is afraid of eating all of his meal at once and who puts something aside for the hard days to come.

In addition, the sages had the following explanation: The three matzot represent Abraham, Isaac and Jacob. Even though the Children of Israel were slaves to Pharaoh in Egypt, they always remembered and held fast to their genealogy.

The three matzot represent the three measures of flour which Abraham told Sarah to bake and to offer the three angels who had arrived at his tent. (Genesis, XVIII,6). According to legend, that day was the 15th day of the month of Nissan.

Dipping Twice

On the evening of the seder, it is customary to dip twice: the first time, the vegetable is dipped in salt water and later, the bitter herbs in the haroseth. Over the centuries, each of these actions has been given symbolic significance.

Bitter Herbs:

The symbolic reason for eating bitter herbs is mentioned in the Torah and in the Passover hagaddah as well. These bitter herbs which we eat, what is the reason for it? For the Egyptians embittered the lives of our fathers in Egypt, as it is written: And they made bitter their lives with hard labor in clay and bricks and in all the works of the field; in all their work they made them serve with severity.

Horseradish is used in the preparation of the bitter herbs. For this, too, the sages also found a special reason: Just as horseradish starts out sweet and its final product is bitter, so did the Egyptians treat our fathers in Egypt.

At first – In the best part of the land settle your father and brothers. (Genesis, XLVII, 6);

And later – And they made bitter their lives with hard labor. (Exodus I, 14).

Haroseth:

This is a combination of fruits and spices mixed with wine.

The symbolic reason for haroseth is that it is a reminder of the clay which our fathers prepared in Egypt.
In the Mishnah it is written that Rabbi Elazar the son of Rabbi Tzadok says that haroseth is a commandment. The sages ask: what is the significance of this commandment? Rabbi Levi says: It is to recall the apple, as it is written: Who is that coming up from the desert, leaning upon her beloved? Under the apple tree did I awaken you (Song of Songs, VIII, 5). This has been interpreted as hinting at the assembling of the People of Israel prior to their leaving Egypt. And Rabbi Yochanan says: In remembrance of the clay, to the making of which the People of Israel were enslaved.   (Psachim CXVI, A, as interpreted by Rabbi Adin Steinsaltz).

The red wine which is mixed in with the haroseth is to recall the blood of the infants who were thrown into the river by order of Pharaoh.

Karpas:

This is a particular vegetable. Potatoes, onions, radishes and similar vegetables can be used for karpas. The significance is interpreted by reversing the order of the Hebrew letters of the word, which yields: 60,000 Israelites worked under severe conditions in Egypt.
The vegetable is eaten in order to whet the curiosity of the young children and to arouse them to ask questions relating to what is happening.

Salt Water:

This symbolizes the tears which our fathers shed in Egypt, as a result of their difficult lives.

As it is written: And the Children of Israel groaned under the weight of their labor, and they called out for help, and their cry under the weight of their labor went up to God. (Exodus II, 23).

Salt water also symbolizes the salty waters of the Red Sea, through which the Children of Israel passed when they came out of Egypt.

The Two Cooked Foods — the Shank Bone and the Egg:

The Commandment of the Paschal Sacrifice:

Two cooked foods are placed on the Passover plate: a shank bone and an egg. These two are in remembrance of the Temple.

A lamb without blemish shall you take, a male one year old, from the sheep or from the goats. And you shall keep it until the 14th day of this month, when the entire assembly of the community of Israel shall slaughter it at twilight.

When the Temple was standing a lamb was sacrificed as a Paschal offering. The sacrifice was offered up on the 14th day of the month of Nissan, during the afternoon hours.

The meat from the sacrifice was eaten on the eve of the 15th. The meat was roasted and then eaten together with the matzot and the bitter herbs. Today, when we no longer offer up Paschal sacrifices, we place a shank bone on the Passover plate in remembrance of the sacrifice.

The egg too, placed on the Passover plate, symbolizes a sacrifice – the festive offering which was eaten before the Paschal sacrifice.

White Clothing

It is customary for the person who conducts the seder to dress in white – a white gown atop his clothes. This whiteness symbolizes the holiday joy. The white garment also symbolizes the holiness of the night's "work." This is similar to the white garments worn by the priests during their holy work in the Temple, as it is written: He shall wear a holy cloth garment. (Leviticus, XVI, 4).

Leaning to One Side

Leaning to one side is one of the more important commandments of the seder eve. In the Mishnah it is written: Even a poor man of Israel shall not begin to eat until he leans over to one side.

It was the custom of free men to lean on cushions as they sat around small tables to eat their meals in comfort.

And Maimonides says: In every generation a man must look upon himself as though he himself has just come out of bondage in Egypt, as it is written: And He

took us from there.... (Deuteronomy VI, 22), and for this the Holy One, Blessed Be He commanded us in the Torah, And you will remember that you were a slave.... (Deuteronomy, V, 15). This means that you yourself were a slave and you came out to freedom and were redeemed. Therefore, when on this night a man dines, he must eat and drink leaning to one side, like a free man.

(Maimonides, Mishneh Torah, The Laws of Hametz and Matzah, Chapter VII).

Elijah the Prophet

It is customary to open the door for Elijah the Prophet when the passage, Pour Out Your Wrath... is recited.

Elijah the Prophet was a prophet of Israel during the reigns of King Ahab and King Ahaziah. He was born in the city of Tishbeh in the Gilead, for which reason he is also called the Tishbi. The Bible speaks of wondrous deeds which Elijah performed during his lifetime. His death, too, was wondrous; he went up to heaven in a whirlwind., riding in a chariot of fire. Jewish tradition believes that Elijah will return and appear once again. In the Book of Malachi it is written that Elijah will make peace between fathers and sons (Malachi III, 23-4). Thus, the belief that Elijah will herald the redemption of Israel when the Messiah comes.

In the Rosh Hashana tractate of the Talmud it is written: In the month of Nissan were we redeemed; in the month of Nissan will we be redeemed in the future. (Rosh Hashana XI, A). Thus, the belief that Elijah, prophet of redemption, will appear on the holiday of redemption.

It is customary to pour a fifth glass of wine, which is called Elijah's cup. Why? There was an argument among the sages as to whether one must drink four glasses of wine — representing the four terms of redemption — or whether it is necessary to drink a fifth glass as well, representing, And I brought [Havaiti], which also is a term of redemption. It was not determined who of the sages was right, and a fifth glass is poured, from which we do not drink, it being argued that when Elijah the Prophet finally comes he will clarify who is correct.

Wheat Money — Passover Flour

During the two weeks preceding Passover, it is customary to collect "wheat money." These are monetary contributions designed to supply the holiday needs of the poor people living in the community where the money is being collected. Whoever so wishes, donates, according to his ability.

Regarding giving, Maimonides says:

Whoever locks the doors of his courtyard and eats and drinks — he and his sons and his wife — and does not feed the poor and the desperate, does not experience the joy of fulfilling a commandment, but only the joy of his gut. The duty of giving is incumbent on everyone. In most communities of the diaspora, a set tax was determined for the Passover Flour Fund.

Selling the Hametz

No leavened bread shall be seen with you and no leaven shall be seen with you in all your territory. (Exodus XIII, 7). Whoever is in possession of hametz and does

Why were They Redeemed from the Land of Egypt?

Four things were responsible for the People of Israel's being redeemed from the Land of Egypt:
That they didn't change their names;
And didn't change their language;
And didn't reveal their secret rites;
And didn't do away with circumcision.

(Midrash Shohar Tov)

not wish to burn it on the eve of Passover, in order not to suffer a loss, is permitted to sell his hametz to a gentile. The buyer and seller both sign an agreement, a document of sale is drawn up and the hametz, though it is sold, remains in the seller's house. Thus, its owner does not violate the prohibition, ...not to be seen and not to be found..., since the hametz belongs to the gentile, not to him.

Nowadays, it is customary for everyone to sell his hametz to the local rabbi, who is granted power of attorney to sell the hametz in his name. The sale is symbolic, and after Passover the hametz returns to its owners.

The Search for Hametz and the Burning of Hametz

It is a biblical commandment to to nullify and get rid of all hametz before the onset of the Passover holiday.

And thus is it written: On the first day, will you rid your house of all leaven. (Exodus, XII,).

The first day — that is the 14th day of the month of Nissan.

Rid your house of all leaven — the meaning is that everyone should nullify the hametz in his heart, think of it as dust, think that he is not in possession of any hametz at all and that any hametz in his possession is no more than dust and something for which he has no need at all. (Maimonides, The Laws of Hametz and Matzah, Chapter II).

However, the sages were not satisfied with a nullification in the heart and also required a search and the removal of all hametz from our surroundings.

...and the writings of the scribes tell us to search for hametz in hidden places and in holes, to examine and to remove it from our territory. And from the writings of the scribes as well, to examine and remove the hametz at night, from the beginning of the evening of the 14th, by candlelight. Since at night everyone is at home, and candlelight is a good light to search by.

(Maimonides, The Laws of hametz and matxah Chapter I, Halacha C).

It would seem at first that the rabbinical regulation requiring the search for hametz, is incomprehensible. If a person thinks of the hametz as dust, why should he look for it in holes and cracks? There are two reasons for this:

The nullification and invalidation depend on a person's thoughts. A situation may arise whereby a person may not abandon his hametz wholeheartedly; therefore, a physical search is required, after which he will remove the hametz from his territory.

In Praise of the People of Israel

Just as with a date palm there is no waste, but dates to eat,
Lulavim out of palm fronds with which to offer praise,
Branches for thatched covering,
Fibers for ropes,
Tendrils for sieves,
An abundance of beams,

from which to build a house -
So is it with the People of Israel:
there is no waste,
But men versed in Scripture,
Men versed in the Mishnah,
Men versed in the Talmud,
Men versed in legends,
Men versed in good deeds,
Men versed in piety.

(Braishith [Genesis] Raba, XLI; Bamidbar [Numbers] Raba, III)

All year long a person is used to using hametz, and even though he may abandon it wholeheartedly, he may, by force of habit, forget the prohibition and eat of it. Therefore, the regulation to search for hametz, to make a careful examination and to remove it from one's territory, before the time comes when eating it is forbidden.

Since on the eve of the holiday the house is clean, it is customary to scatter 10 pieces of bread in various places throughout the house, in order to ensure that hametz will be found during the search. It is customary to use a feather when searching, since it is capable of getting into holes and cracks.

The hametz which is found during the search, together with that which has been set aside for eating the following morning, is held together in a bundle, so that the crumbs do not scatter all over the house again. The next morning the hametz is burned.

The Search for Hametz – A Symbol of Freedom

The Exodus of the Children of Israel from slavery to freedom was bound up with the injunction that they take upon themselves responsibility for their deeds. This is what is symbolized by hametz and matzah.

The first 13 days of the month of Nissan hint at the first 13 years of a man's life, before his bar mitzvah, with each day representing a year. On the eve of the 14th day, i.e., on the first night of the 14th year, when a man takes upon himself the responsibilities of the commandments, the "hametz" is searched for.

(Rabbi Haim Vital, The Book of Intentions).

Just as entry into adulthood entails responsibility, so does the hametz entail the taking of responsibility, to burn it.

The Process of Searching for Leaven (Hametz)

On the eve of the 14th day of Nissan, after nightfall, a search for leaven is carried out. Before the search, a blessing is recited:
After the search, the following is recited:
Any and all leaven and yeast in my possession, which I didn't see, or perceive or burn, and which is unknown to me – may it be nullified and ownerless, like the dust of the land.

The Process of Burning the Leaven

On the eve of Passover, on the morning of the 14th of Nissan, the crumbs of leaven which were gathered up the previous evening are burnt, together with all the leaven left in the house. After burning the leaven, the following is recited: Any and all leaven and yeast in my possession, which I saw or didn't see, perceived or didn't perceive, burnt or didn't burn – may it be nullified and ownerless, like the dust of the land.

A complete matzah is taken, together with an olive-sized quantity of meat, egg, or any cooked food. This is placed atop the matzah,

and the following is recited: With this overlapping,
may we be permitted to carry over baking, cooking, keeping food warm, lighting
candles and performing whatever is necessary, from the holiday to the Sabbath –
we and everyone else dwelling in this city.
If the holiday eve falls on an ordinary day of the week, the following is recited:
If the holiday eve falls on the Sabbath, the following is recited:

THE K'ARAH OR PASSOVER DISH

Three matzot are placed in the k'arah.
Upon them are placed a shankbone on the right; a hard-boiled egg on the left; bitter herbs in the middle; haroseth below the shankbone on the right; a vegetable (parsley, celery, a potato, etc.) below the hard-boiled egg on the left; and hazeret (another vegetable) at the bottom under the bitter herbs.

קְעָרַת הַסֵּדֶר

שָׂמִים שָׁלוֹשׁ מַצּוֹת: כֹּהֵן, לֵוִי וְיִשְׂרָאֵל. בְּצַד יָמִין זְרוֹעַ וְתַחְתֶּיהָ חֲרֹסֶת, בֵּיצָה מִשְּׂמֹאל וְתַחְתֶּיהָ כַּרְפַּס, וּבֵינֵיהֶם — מָרוֹר.

זְרוֹעַ • בֵּיצָה • מָרוֹר • חֲרֹסֶת • כַּרְפַּס

The Seas of the Land of Israel

Rabbi Yochanan said: what is the meaning of that which is written, For He, on the seas has founded it and established it upon the rivers. (Psalms XXIV, 2)
These are the seven seas and four rivers which surround the Land of Israel:
The sea of Tiberias [the Sea of Galilee];
The sea of Sodom [the Dead Sea];
The sea of Hulat [the Sea of Hula];
The sea of Shalit [the reference is unclear];
And the sea of Samkhu [which was appended to the Dead Sea]
And the sea of Apamya [located in Syria];
And the Great Sea [the Mediterranean Sea].
The four rivers — the Jordan, the Yarmukh, the Carmion and the Pigah.

(Baba Batra, LXXIV, B)

ORDER OF THE SEDER SERVICE   סִימָנֵי הַסֵּדֶר

Kiddush   The wine is blessed.

קַדֵּשׁ – מְקַדְּשִׁים עַל הַיַּיִן.

Washing the hands   The hands are washed before the vegetable is eaten.

וּרְחַץ – נוֹטְלִים יָדַיִם לִפְנֵי אֲכִילַת כַּרְפַּס.

Karpas   The vegetable is eaten.

כַּרְפַּס – אוֹכְלִים אֶת הַכַּרְפַּס.

Dividing the matzah   The middle matzah is broken, with the larger of its two pieces being set aside as the Afikoman.

יַחַץ – חוֹצִים אֶת הַמַּצָּה הָאֶמְצָעִית, מַצְפִּינִים לַאֲפִיקוֹמָן.

Reciting the Haggadah   The hagaddah is recited.

מַגִּיד – אוֹמְרִים אֶת הַהַגָּדָה.

Washing the hands   The hands are washed before the evening meal, and a blessing is recited.

רָחְצָה – נוֹטְלִים יָדַיִם לִפְנֵי הָאֲרוּחָה וּמְבָרְכִים.

The blessing over bread   A blessing is recited over the matzah – as though it were bread.

מוֹצִיא – מְבָרְכִים עַל הַמַּצָּה – כְּמוֹ עַל לֶחֶם.

The blessing of the matzah   A special blessing for the eating of matzah is recited.

מַצָּה – מְבָרְכִים בְּרָכָה מְיֻחֶדֶת עַל אֲכִילַת מַצָּה.

The bitter herb   The bitter herbs are eaten.

מָרוֹר – אוֹכְלִים מָרוֹר.

The matzah with the bitter herb
Matzah and bitter herbs are eaten together in a sandwich.

כּוֹרֵךְ – אוֹכְלִים מַצָּה וּמָרוֹר כְּשֶׁהֵם כְּרוּכִים יַחַד.

The meal   The holiday meal is eaten.

שֻׁלְחָן עוֹרֵךְ – אוֹכְלִים אֶת סְעוּדַת הַחַג.

The Afikoman   The Afikoman, which was hidden at the start of the Seder, is eaten.

צָפוּן – אוֹכְלִים מֵהָאֲפִיקוֹמָן שֶׁהִצְפַּן בִּתְחִלַּת הַסֵּדֶר.

Grace after the meal   Grace after the meal, is recited.

בָּרֵךְ – מְבָרְכִים עַל הַמָּזוֹן שֶׁאָכַלְנוּ.

Hallel   The prayer of thanksgiving (Hallel) is recited.

הַלֵּל – אוֹמְרִים אֶת תְּפִלַּת הַהַלֵּל.

All accepted! The conclusion of the Seder – in the hope that it was accepted willingly, and that we too are satisfied.

נִרְצָה – סִיּוּם הַסֵּדֶר.
מְקֻוִּים שֶׁהוּא הִתְקַבֵּל בְּרָצוֹן וְגַם אָנוּ מְרֻצִּים.

בורא פרי הגפן

Cabbage in the Land of Israel

Rabbi Shimon ben Halafta said:
Our father left us a cabbage stalk, and we had to take a ladder to it.

(Ketuboth, CXI, B)

The Riches of the Land of Israel

Rabbi Hiya bar Ada used to teach Raish Lakish's young children:
He was absent for three days and didn't show up.
When he finally came Raish Lakish said to him: What was the cause of your absence?
He said: My father left me a grape vine. On the first day I harvested 300 clusters; on the second day I harvested 300 clusters; on the third day I harvested 300 clusters... and I had to leave unharvested more than half of the vine.

(Ketuboth, CXI)

קַדֵשׁ

The first cup of wine is poured

All drink the first cup while leaning to the left.

Kiddush

If the night of the Seder falls on Friday evening, the text is recited from here:

(Genesis 1:31 – 2:3) And it was evening, and it was morning the sixth day. And the heavens and the earth were finished, and all their host. And on the seventh day God ended His work which He had made; and He rested on the seventh day from all His work which He had made. And God blessed the seventh day, and sanctified it; because in it He rested from all His work which God created to function.

Blessed are You, O Lord our God, King of the Universe, Creator of the fruit of the vine.

קַדֵּשׁ

מוֹזְגִים כּוֹס יַיִן מְלֵאָה לְקִדּוּשׁ. זוֹהִי הַכּוֹס הָרִאשׁוֹנָה מִתּוֹךְ אַרְבַּע הַכּוֹסוֹת. מְקַדְּשִׁים וְשׁוֹתִים בַּהֲסִבַּת שְׂמֹאל.

אוֹמְרִים: הִנְנִי מוּכָן וּמְזֻמָּן לְקַיֵּם מִצְוַת כּוֹס רִאשׁוֹן מֵאַרְבַּע כּוֹסוֹת לְשֵׁם יִחוּד קֻדְשָׁא בְּרִיךְ הוּא וּשְׁכִינְתֵּהּ, עַל יְדֵי הַהוּא טָמִיר וְנֶעֱלָם בְּשֵׁם כָּל יִשְׂרָאֵל.

קִדּוּשׁ שֶׁל פֶּסַח

אִם לֵיל הַסֵּדֶר חָל בְּלֵיל שַׁבָּת מַתְחִילִים:

(בְּלַחַשׁ) וַיְהִי עֶרֶב וַיְהִי בֹקֶר (בְּקוֹל) יוֹם הַשִּׁשִּׁי. וַיְכֻלּוּ הַשָּׁמַיִם וְהָאָרֶץ וְכָל צְבָאָם. וַיְכַל אֱלֹדִים בַּיּוֹם הַשְּׁבִיעִי מְלַאכְתּוֹ אֲשֶׁר עָשָׂה, וַיִּשְׁבֹּת בַּיּוֹם הַשְּׁבִיעִי מִכָּל מְלַאכְתּוֹ אֲשֶׁר עָשָׂה. וַיְבָרֶךְ אֱלֹהִים אֶת יוֹם הַשְּׁבִיעִי וַיְקַדֵּשׁ אֹתוֹ, כִּי בוֹ שָׁבַת מִכָּל מְלַאכְתּוֹ, אֲשֶׁר בָּרָא אֱלֹהִים לַעֲשׂוֹת: (בְּרֵאשִׁית ב, א-ב)

סַבְרִי מָרָנָן

בָּרוּךְ אַתָּה יְיָ אֱלֹהֵינוּ מֶלֶךְ הָעוֹלָם בּוֹרֵא פְּרִי הַגָּפֶן.

מְנוֹרֵא בְּרִי הַגָּפֶן

The Land of Israel – A Unique Land

It is unlike the Land of Egypt -
The Land of Egypt drinks of its own water;
The Land of Israel drinks rain water.
The lowlands of the Land of Egypt drink
water, the highlands do not drink;
In the Land of Israel, both the highlands
and lowlands do drink.
In the Land of Egypt, the visible land drinks,
the hidden land does not drink;
In the Land of Israel, both the visible and
hidden lands drink.
First the Land of Egypt drinks and then
it is sowed;
The Land of Israel drinks and is sowed,
is sowed and drinks.
The Land of Egypt does nor drink every day;
The Land of Israel drinks every day.
If those who work the Land of Egypt do not
toil over it with chisel and axe and lose sleep
over it, it will provide them with nothing;
But this is not true of the Land of Israel -
Those who work it go to sleep in their own
beds and God brings them rain.

(Yalkut Shimoni to Akev)

On Friday night begin the kiddush by reciting the following paragraph.

Blessed are You, O Lord our God, King of the Universe, who has chosen us from all peoples, and has exalted us above all tongues, and has sanctified us by your commandments. And You have given us, O Lord our God, in love, *(Sabbaths for rest and)* anniversaries for rejoicing, festivals and seasons for gladness; this *(Sabbath day and this)* Feast of Matzot, the season of our freedom, *(in love)*, a holy convocation, a memorial of our departure from Egypt. For You have chosen us, and sanctified us above all peoples; and You have given us as heritage Your holy *(Sabbath and)* seasons *(in love and in favor)*, in joy and in gladness. Blessed are You, O Lord, who sanctified *(the Sabbath and)* Israel and the festive seasons.

Everyone drinks the wine.

בָּרוּךְ אַתָּה יְיָ מְקַדֵּשׁ הַשַּׁבָּת

בָּרוּךְ אַתָּה יְיָ אֱלֹהֵינוּ מֶלֶךְ הָעוֹלָם אֲשֶׁר בָּחַר בָּנוּ מִכָּל עָם וְרוֹמְמָנוּ מִכָּל לָשׁוֹן וְקִדְּשָׁנוּ בְּמִצְוֹתָיו. וַתִּתֶּן לָנוּ יְיָ אֱלֹהֵינוּ בְּאַהֲבָה שַׁבָּתוֹת לִמְנוּחָה וּמוֹעֲדִים לְשִׂמְחָה, חַגִּים וּזְמַנִּים לְשָׂשׂוֹן אֶת יוֹם הַשַּׁבָּת הַזֶּה וְאֶת יוֹם חַג הַמַּצוֹת הַזֶּה זְמַן חֵרוּתֵנוּ בְּאַהֲבָה מִקְרָא קֹדֶשׁ זֵכֶר לִיצִיאַת מִצְרָיִם. כִּי בָנוּ בָחַרְתָּ וְאוֹתָנוּ קִדַּשְׁתָּ מִכָּל הָעַמִּים וְשַׁבָּת וּמוֹעֲדֵי קָדְשֶׁךָ בְּאַהֲבָה וּבְרָצוֹן בְּשִׂמְחָה וּבְשָׂשׂוֹן הִנְחַלְתָּנוּ.

בָּרוּךְ אַתָּה יְיָ מְקַדֵּשׁ הַשַּׁבָּת וְיִשְׂרָאֵל וְהַזְּמַנִּים.

בָּרוּךְ אַתָּה יְיָ אֱלֹהֵינוּ מֶלֶךְ הָעוֹלָם שֶׁהֶחֱיָנוּ וְקִיְּמָנוּ וְהִגִּיעָנוּ לַזְּמַן הַזֶּה.

כֻּלָּם שׁוֹתִים אֶת כּוֹס הַיַּיִן.

נוסְעִים לְבֵן
יָמִים בַּמִּדְבָּר

The kiddush concludes with:

Blessed are You, O Lord our God, King of the Universe, who has preserved us and sustained us and enabled us to reach this season.

All drink the first cup while leaning to the left.

On Saturday night add the following paragraph:

Blessed are You, O Lord our God, King of the Universe, Creator of the light of fire. Blessed are You, O Lord our God, King of the Universe, who makes distinction between holy and profane, between light and darkness, between Israel and the nations, between the seventh day and the six days of toil. You have made distinction between the sanctity of the Sabbath and the sanctity of the festival, and have sanctified the seventh day above the six days of toil; You have distinguished and sanctified Your people Israel with Your own sanctity. Blessed are You, O Lord, who makes distinction between holy and holy.

The kiddush concludes with:

Blessed are You, O Lord our God, King of the Universe, who has preserved us and sustained us and enabled us to reach this season.

The Saturday night Kiddush is a combination of Kiddush and Havdalah.

אִם לֵיל הַסֵּדֶר חָל בְּיוֹם חֹל, מַתְחִילִים:

סַבְרִי מָרָנָן וְרַבָּנָן וְרַבּוֹתַי

בָּרוּךְ אַתָּה יְיָ, אֱלֹהֵינוּ מֶלֶךְ הָעוֹלָם, בּוֹרֵא פְּרִי הַגָּפֶן.

בָּרוּךְ אַתָּה יְיָ, אֱלֹהֵינוּ מֶלֶךְ הָעוֹלָם, אֲשֶׁר בָּחַר בָּנוּ מִכָּל עָם, וְרוֹמְמָנוּ מִכָּל לָשׁוֹן, וְקִדְּשָׁנוּ בְּמִצְוֹתָיו, וַתִּתֶּן־לָנוּ, יְיָ אֱלֹהֵינוּ, בְּאַהֲבָה מוֹעֲדִים לְשִׂמְחָה, חַגִּים וּזְמַנִּים לְשָׂשׂוֹן, אֶת יוֹם חַג הַמַּצּוֹת הַזֶּה, זְמַן חֵרוּתֵנוּ מִקְרָא קֹדֶשׁ, זֵכֶר לִיצִיאַת מִצְרָיִם. כִּי בָנוּ בָחַרְתָּ וְאוֹתָנוּ קִדַּשְׁתָּ מִכָּל הָעַמִּים, וּמוֹעֲדֵי קָדְשֶׁךָ בְּשִׂמְחָה וּבְשָׂשׂוֹן הִנְחַלְתָּנוּ. בָּרוּךְ אַתָּה יְיָ, מְקַדֵּשׁ יִשְׂרָאֵל וְהַזְּמַנִּים.

בָּרוּךְ אַתָּה יְיָ, אֱלֹהֵינוּ מֶלֶךְ הָעוֹלָם, שֶׁהֶחֱיָנוּ וְקִיְּמָנוּ וְהִגִּיעָנוּ לַזְּמַן הַזֶּה.

כֻּלָּם שׁוֹתִים אֶת כּוֹס הַיַּיִן.

אִם לֵיל הַסֵּדֶר חָל בְּמוֹצָאֵי שַׁבָּת, אוֹמְרִים:

סַבְרִי מָרָנָן

בָּרוּךְ אַתָּה יְיָ אֱלֹהֵינוּ מֶלֶךְ הָעוֹלָם בּוֹרֵא פְּרִי הַגָּפֶן.

בָּרוּךְ אַתָּה יְיָ אֱלֹהֵינוּ מֶלֶךְ הָעוֹלָם אֲשֶׁר בָּחַר בָּנוּ מִכָּל עָם וְרוֹמְמָנוּ מִכָּל לָשׁוֹן וְקִדְּשָׁנוּ בְּמִצְוֹתָיו. וַתִּתֶּן לָנוּ יְיָ אֱלֹהֵינוּ בְּאַהֲבָה מוֹעֲדִים לְשִׂמְחָה חַגִּים וּזְמַנִּים לְשָׂשׂוֹן אֶת יוֹם חַג הַמַּצּוֹת הַזֶּה זְמַן חֵרוּתֵנוּ מִקְרָא קֹדֶשׁ זֵכֶר לִיצִיאַת מִצְרָיִם. כִּי בָנוּ בָחַרְתָּ וְאוֹתָנוּ קִדַּשְׁתָּ מִכָּל הָעַמִּים וּמוֹעֲדֵי קָדְשֶׁךָ בְּשִׂמְחָה וּבְשָׂשׂוֹן הִנְחַלְתָּנוּ.

בָּרוּךְ אַתָּה יְיָ מְקַדֵּשׁ יִשְׂרָאֵל וְהַזְּמַנִּים.

בָּרוּךְ אַתָּה יְיָ, אֱלֹהֵינוּ מֶלֶךְ הָעוֹלָם, בּוֹרֵא מְאוֹרֵי הָאֵשׁ.

בָּרוּךְ אַתָּה יְיָ, אֱלֹהֵינוּ מֶלֶךְ הָעוֹלָם, הַמַּבְדִּיל בֵּין קֹדֶשׁ לְחֹל, בֵּין אוֹר לְחֹשֶׁךְ, בֵּין יִשְׂרָאֵל לָעַמִּים, בֵּין יוֹם הַשְּׁבִיעִי לְשֵׁשֶׁת יְמֵי הַמַּעֲשֶׂה; בֵּין קְדֻשַּׁת שַׁבָּת לִקְדֻשַּׁת יוֹם־טוֹב הִבְדַּלְתָּ, וְאֶת יוֹם הַשְּׁבִיעִי מִשֵּׁשֶׁת יְמֵי הַמַּעֲשֶׂה קִדַּשְׁתָּ; הִבְדַּלְתָּ וְקִדַּשְׁתָּ אֶת עַמְּךָ יִשְׂרָאֵל בִּקְדֻשָּׁתֶךָ. בָּרוּךְ אַתָּה יְיָ, הַמַּבְדִּיל בֵּין קֹדֶשׁ לְקֹדֶשׁ.

בָּרוּךְ אַתָּה יְיָ אֱלֹהֵינוּ מֶלֶךְ הָעוֹלָם, שֶׁהֶחֱיָנוּ וְקִיְּמָנוּ וְהִגִּיעָנוּ לַזְּמַן הַזֶּה.

כֻּלָּם שׁוֹתִים אֶת כּוֹס הַיַּיִן.

בְּמוֹצָאֵי שַׁבָּת יֵשׁ בְּקִדּוּשׁ עַל הַיַּיִן מֶזֶג שֶׁל "קִדּוּשׁ" וְ"הַבְדָּלָה".

A Lamp & Olive Branches

Rabbi Aha said: The People of Israel may be compared to an olive tree, as it is written: The Lord has called you a fresh olive tree, fair with lovely fruit. (Jeremiah, XI, 16)
And the Holy One, Blessed Be He may be compared to a candle, and together they give off a single light.
Thus, the Holy One, Blessed Be He said to the People of Israel:
Since My light is your light and your light is My light — you and I will go together to illuminate Zion.

(Psikta Rabati)

וּרְחַץ

The celebrants wash their hands but do not say the customary blessing.

נוֹטְלִים יָדַיִם וְאֵין מְבָרְכִים אֶת הַבְּרָכָה הַמְיֻחֶדֶת: "עַל נְטִילַת יָדַיִם".

כַּרְפַּס

All take a vegetable, dip it in salt water and recite the following blessing:

לוֹקְחִים מְעַט כַּרְפַּס, פָּחוֹת מִכַּזַּיִת, טוֹבְלִים אוֹתוֹ בְּמֵי מֶלַח אוֹ בְּחֹמֶץ וּמְבָרְכִים עָלָיו:
בָּרוּךְ אַתָּה יְיָ, אֱלֹהֵינוּ מֶלֶךְ הָעוֹלָם, בּוֹרֵא פְּרִי הָאֲדָמָה.
אוֹכְלִים מִן הַכַּרְפַּס.

יַחַץ

Blessed are You, O Lord our God,

King of the Universe,

Creator of the Produce of the Earth.

The middle of the three matzot on the Passover plate is broken in two. The larger part is hidden as the Afikoman and the smaller part is returned to its place on the plate.

בּוֹצְעִים אֶת הַמַּצָּה הָאֶמְצָעִית מִשָּׁלוֹשׁ הַמַּצּוֹת הַמֻּנָּחוֹת עַל הַקְּעָרָה, לִשְׁנַיִם. מַצְפִּינִים אֶת הַחֵלֶק הַגָּדוֹל לַאֲפִיקוֹמָן, וְאֶת הַחֵלֶק הַקָּטָן מַשְׁאִירִים בֵּין הַמַּצּוֹת שֶׁעַל הַקְּעָרָה.
(אֲפִיקוֹמָן הוּא מִלָּה אֲרָמִית וְאַחַת מִמַּשְׁמְעֻיּוֹתֶיהָ: לִפְתָּן שֶׁלְּאַחַר הָאֲרוּחָה.)

Rise Up, Awaken, for a Guest has Arrived

Rise up, awaken, for a guest has arrived. (Isaiah, LX, 1)
Rabbi Yochanan said: A comparison can be made to someone who is walking along the road at twilight time.
Someone else came along and lit a candle — and it was extinguished.
Then someone else came along and lit a candle — and it was extinguished.
He said: from now on I'll wait for the morning light only.
This is what the People of Israel said to the Holy One, Blessed Be He:
During Moses' time we built You a lamp — and it was extinguished;
During Solomon's time — and it was extinguished;
From now on, we will wait for Your light alone.
And thus, the Holy One, Blessed Be He said: Rise up, awaken, for a guest has arrived....

(Psikta Rabati)

מַגִּיד

The head of the household uncovers the matzot, raises the k'arah and says:

This is the bread of affliction that our fathers ate in the land of Egypt. All who are hungry – let them come and eat; all who are needy – let them come and celebrate the Passover. Now we are here, but next year may we be free men!

The head of the household puts the k'arah back.

מְגַלִּים אֶת הַמַּצּוֹת, מַגְבִּיהִים אֶת הַקְּעָרָה וְיֵשׁ נוֹהֲגִים לוֹמַר:

הִנְנִי מוּכָן וּמְזֻמָּן לְקַיֵּם הַמִּצְוָה לְסַפֵּר בִּיצִיאַת מִצְרַיִם לְשֵׁם יִחוּד קֻדְשָׁא בְּרִיךְ הוּא וּשְׁכִינְתֵּהּ, עַל יְדֵי הַהוּא טָמִיר וְנֶעְלָם בְּשֵׁם כָּל יִשְׂרָאֵל.

הַסְּפָרַדִים אוֹמְרִים: בִּבְהִילוּ יָצָאנוּ מִמִּצְרַיִם. ("בְּבְהִילוּ" הוּא הַתַּרְגּוּם הָאֲרַמִי לְמִלָּה לְ"בְּחִפָּזוֹן".)

הָא לַחְמָא עַנְיָא

דִּי אֲכַלוּ אֲבָהָתַנָא בְּאַרְעָא דְמִצְרָיִם. כָּל דִּכְפִין יֵיתֵי וְיֵכֹל, כָּל דִּצְרִיךְ יֵיתֵי וְיִפְסַח. הָשַׁתָּא הָכָא, לְשָׁנָה הַבָּאָה בְּאַרְעָא דְיִשְׂרָאֵל. הָשַׁתָּא עַבְדֵי,

The Land of Israel — A Comely Land

There are people who are comely, but whose dress is repugnant.
And repugnant people, whose dress is comely.
And the People of Israel, whom the land finds comely and who are comely to the land.

(Bamidbar [Numbers] Raba, XXIII, 5)

The second cup of wine is poured and the youngest child asks the "Four Questions".

HOW IS THIS NIGHT DIFFERENT
FROM ALL OTHER NIGHTS?

On all other nights, we may eat either leavened bread or matzah, but on this night only matzah;
on all other nights we may eat other kinds of vegetables, but on this night bitter herbs:
on all other nights we need not dip our herbs even once, but on this night we do so twice:
on all other nights we eat either sitting upright or reclining,
but on this night we all recline.

מוֹזְגִים כּוֹס שְׁנִיָּה, וְהַבֵּן הַצָּעִיר בַּמִּשְׁפָּחָה שׁוֹאֵל אֶת הַקֻּשִׁיוֹת:

הַלַּיְלָה הַזֶּה מִכָּל הַלֵּילוֹת?
שֶׁבְּכָל הַלֵּילוֹת אָנוּ אוֹכְלִין חָמֵץ וּמַצָּה, הַלַּיְלָה הַזֶּה כֻּלּוֹ מַצָּה;
שֶׁבְּכָל הַלֵּילוֹת אָנוּ אוֹכְלִין שְׁאָר יְרָקוֹת, הַלַּיְלָה הַזֶּה מָרוֹר;
שֶׁבְּכָל הַלֵּילוֹת אֵין אָנוּ מַטְבִּילִין אֲפִלּוּ פַּעַם אֶחָת, הַלַּיְלָה הַזֶּה שְׁתֵּי פְעָמִים;
שֶׁבְּכָל הַלֵּילוֹת אָנוּ אוֹכְלִין בֵּין יוֹשְׁבִין וּבֵין מְסֻבִּין, הַלַּיְלָה הַזֶּה כֻּלָּנוּ מְסֻבִּין.

37

The Land of Israel — Better than all Other Lands

For the land to which you are going, to inherit it, is not like the land of Egypt, from which you have departed, where you sowed your seed and watered the land with your feet, like a garden of vegetables:

And the land to which you are moving, to inherit it, is a land of hills and valleys, which drinks of the rainfall coming down from the sky.

A land which the Lord your God keeps watch over; the eyes of the Lord your God are on it always, from the first day of the new year, until the last.

(Deuteronomy, XI, 10-12)

The head of the household uncovers the matzot and says:

"We were Pharaoh's bondmen in Egypt;

עֲבָדִים הָיִינוּ לְפַרְעֹה בְּמִצְרַיִם

and the Lord our God brought us out therefrom with a mighty hand" *(Deut. 6:21)* and an outstretched arm. Now if the Holy One, blessed be He, had not brought our fathers forth from Egypt, then we, and our children, and our children's children, would be servants to Pharaoh in Egypt. Therefore, even were we all wise, all men of understanding, all advanced in years, and all endowed with knowledge of the Torah, it would nevertheless be our duty to tell the story of the coming forth from Egypt; and the more a person dwells on the exodus from Egypt, the more praiseworthy he is to be considered.

מְכַלִּים אֶת הַמַּצּוֹת וְאוֹמְרִים:

עֲבָדִים הָיִינוּ לְפַרְעֹה בְּמִצְרַיִם, וַיּוֹצִיאֵנוּ יְיָ אֱלֹהֵינוּ מִשָּׁם, בְּיָד חֲזָקָה, וּבִזְרוֹעַ נְטוּיָה. וְאִלּוּ לֹא הוֹצִיא הַקָּדוֹשׁ בָּרוּךְ הוּא אֶת אֲבוֹתֵינוּ מִמִּצְרַיִם, הֲרֵי אָנוּ וּבָנֵינוּ וּבְנֵי בָנֵינוּ, מְשֻׁעְבָּדִים הָיִינוּ לְפַרְעֹה בְּמִצְרַיִם. וַאֲפִלּוּ כֻּלָּנוּ חֲכָמִים, כֻּלָּנוּ נְבוֹנִים, כֻּלָּנוּ זְקֵנִים, כֻּלָּנוּ יוֹדְעִים אֶת הַתּוֹרָה – מִצְוָה עָלֵינוּ לְסַפֵּר בִּיצִיאַת מִצְרַיִם, וְכָל הַמַּרְבֶּה לְסַפֵּר בִּיצִיאַת מִצְרַיִם הֲרֵי זֶה מְשֻׁבָּח.

Places in the Land of Israel which were Purchased for Cash

Three places exist, regarding which the nations of the world cannot trick the People of Israel by claiming, you possess stolen property. And these are:

The Cave of Machpelah, the Temple and Joseph's burial plot.

As to the Cave of Machpelah, it is written, And Abraham heeded the words of Efron, and Abraham weighed out the money for Efron.... (Genesis, XXIII, 16)

As to the Temple, it is written, And on the spot David gave shekels of gold to Arnon....
(I Chronicles, XXI, 25)

As to Joseph's burial plot, it is written, And Joseph's remains, which the Children of Israel brought up from Egypt, were buried in Schehem, on a plot of ground which Jacob had purchased. (Joshua, XXIV, 32)

(Braishith [Genesis] Raba, LXXIX, 7)

It is told of Rabbi Eliezer, Rabbi Joshua, Rabbi Elazar, son of Azariah, Rabbi Akiva, and Rabbi Tarfon, that they were once reclining at Bnei Brak and were recounting the story of the coming forth from Egypt all that night, until their pupils came and said to them: "Our Masters! The time has come for reciting the **shema** prayer of the morning."
Rabbi Elazar b. Azariah, said: "I am as one of seventy years of age, yet I was not able to convince my colleagues to have the exodus from Egypt told at night until Ben Zoma explained it: It is said, "That you may remember the day when you came forth from the land of Egypt all the days of your life" *(Deut. 16:3)*. "The days of your life" would imply only the days; "All the days of your life" includes the nights also. The Sages, however, expound it as follows:

"The days of your life" refers to this world; "All the days of your life" is to include the days of the Messiah."
Blessed be the All-Present, blessed be He; Blessed be He who gave the Torah to His people Israel, blessed be He.

מַעֲשֶׂה

בְּרַבִּי אֱלִיעֶזֶר, וְרַבִּי יְהוֹשֻׁעַ, וְרַבִּי אֶלְעָזָר בֶּן־עֲזַרְיָה, וְרַבִּי עֲקִיבָא, וְרַבִּי טַרְפוֹן, שֶׁהָיוּ מְסֻבִּין בִּבְנֵי־בְרַק, וְהָיוּ מְסַפְּרִים
בִּיצִיאַת מִצְרַיִם כָּל אוֹתוֹ הַלַּיְלָה, עַד שֶׁבָּאוּ תַלְמִידֵיהֶם וְאָמְרוּ לָהֶם:
רַבּוֹתֵינוּ, הִגִּיעַ זְמַן קְרִיאַת שְׁמַע שֶׁל שַׁחֲרִית.

אָמַר רַבִּי אֶלְעָזָר בֶּן־עֲזַרְיָה: הֲרֵי אֲנִי כְּבֶן שִׁבְעִים שָׁנָה וְלֹא זָכִיתִי שֶׁתֵּאָמֵר יְצִיאַת מִצְרַיִם בַּלֵּילוֹת, עַד שֶׁדְּרָשָׁהּ בֶּן־זוֹמָא,
שֶׁנֶּאֱמַר (דְּבָרִים טז, ג): "לְמַעַן תִּזְכֹּר אֶת יוֹם צֵאתְךָ מֵאֶרֶץ מִצְרַיִם כֹּל יְמֵי חַיֶּיךָ". "יְמֵי חַיֶּיךָ" – הַיָּמִים, "כֹּל יְמֵי חַיֶּיךָ" – הַלֵּילוֹת.
וַחֲכָמִים אוֹמְרִים: "יְמֵי חַיֶּיךָ" – הָעוֹלָם הַזֶּה, "כֹּל יְמֵי חַיֶּיךָ" – לְהָבִיא לִימוֹת הַמָּשִׁיחַ.

בָּרוּךְ

הַמָּקוֹם, בָּרוּךְ הוּא, בָּרוּךְ שֶׁנָּתַן תּוֹרָה לְעַמּוֹ יִשְׂרָאֵל, בָּרוּךְ הוּא.

The Land of Israel — A Fertile Land

For the Lord your God is bringing you to a good land, a land of brooks, of fountains and springs, flowing out from valleys and hills.

A land of wheat and barley, of grapevines, figs and pomegranates, a land of olive oil and date honey, a land in which you will eat bread without indigence, in which you will lack nothing, a land whose stones are iron and out of whose hills copper can be mined. And you will eat and be full and bless the Lord your God for the good land He has given you.

(Deuteronomy, VIII, 7-11)

THE TORAH SPEAKS WITH REFERENCE TO FOUR SONS:

ONE WISE,
ONE WICKED,
ONE SIMPLE,
AND ONE WHO DOES NOT KNOW
HOW TO ASK.

THE WISE SON

– what does he say? "What is the meaning of the testimonies and the statutes and the judgements which the Lord our God has commanded you?" *(Deut. 6:20)* You must expound to him (all) the laws of the Passover, *(to the very last law, that)* we may not eat anything after the paschal sacrifice.

THE WICKED SON

– what does he say? "What is this service to you?" *(Ex. 12:26)* "You," he insinuates, not himself. Since he has excluded himself from the community, he has denied a cardinal principle. Therefore blunt his teeth, and say, "It is because of that which the Lord did for me when I came forth from Egypt" *(Ex. 13:8)*: for me, not for him – for if he had been there, he would not have been redeemed!

THE SIMPLE SON

– what does he say? "What is this?" *(Ex. 13:14)*. And you shall say unto him, "By the strength of *(His)* hand the Lord brought us out of the Land of Egypt, from the house of bondage" *(ibid.)*.

כְּנֶגֶד אַרְבָּעָה בָנִים דִּבְּרָה תוֹרָה:

אֶחָד **חָכָם**, וְאֶחָד **רָשָׁע**, וְאֶחָד **תָּם**, וְאֶחָד שֶׁאֵינוֹ יוֹדֵעַ לִשְׁאֹל.

חָכָם

מָה הוּא אוֹמֵר? "מָה הָעֵדֹת וְהַחֻקִּים וְהַמִּשְׁפָּטִים, אֲשֶׁר צִוָּה יְיָ אֱלֹהֵינוּ אֶתְכֶם?" (דְּבָרִים ו, כ) וְאַף אַתָּה אֱמָר-לוֹ כְּהִלְכוֹת הַפֶּסַח: "אֵין מַפְטִירִין אַחַר הַפֶּסַח אֲפִיקוֹמָן".

רָשָׁע

מָה הוּא אוֹמֵר? "מָה הָעֲבֹדָה הַזֹּאת לָכֶם?" (שְׁמוֹת יב, כו) "לָכֶם" וְלֹא לוֹ! וּלְפִי שֶׁהוֹצִיא אֶת עַצְמוֹ מִן הַכְּלָל, וְכָפַר בָּעִקָּר, אַף אַתָּה הַקְהֵה אֶת שִׁנָּיו וֶאֱמָר-לוֹ: "בַּעֲבוּר זֶה עָשָׂה יְיָ לִי בְּצֵאתִי מִמִּצְרָיִם". (שְׁמוֹת יג, ח) "לִי" וְלֹא לוֹ. אִלּוּ הָיָה שָׁם, לֹא הָיָה נִגְאָל.

תָּם

מָה הוּא אוֹמֵר? "מַה זֹּאת?" "וְאָמַרְתָּ אֵלָיו: בְּחֹזֶק יָד הוֹצִיאָנוּ יְיָ מִמִּצְרַיִם מִבֵּית עֲבָדִים". (שְׁמוֹת יג, יד)

The Land of Israel — A Dear Land

[This verse comes] to inform you that there is nothing so dear as the Land of Israel.
Said the Holy One, Blessed Be He, to Moses: In truth, the land is dear to Me, as it is
written, A land which the Lord your God inquires after ceaselessly. (Deuteronomy XI)
And: the People of Israel are dear to Me, as it is written, Because the Lord loves you.
(Deuteronomy VII)

Said the Holy One, Blessed Be He, I am taking the People of Israel, who are dear to Me, into
the Land of Israel, which is dear to Me, as it is written, For you are going to the land of Canaan.

(Bamidbar [Numbers] Raba, XXIII, 7)

AS FOR HIM WHO DOES NOT KNOW HOW TO ASK,

you shall yourself begin for him, as it is said: "And you shall tell your son in that day, saying, It is because of that which the Lord did for me when I came forth from Egypt."
(Ex. 13:8)

One might think that this exposition (of the story of the exodus) should begin from the New Moon of Nissan. The text says, however, "In that day." If it is to be (expounded) "in that day," it might be thought that this should begin in the daytime; but the text says "because of that." "Because of **that**" implies the time when matzah and bitter herbs are laid before you.

וְשֶׁאֵינוֹ

יוֹדֵעַ לִשְׁאֹל, אַתְּ פְּתַח לוֹ, שֶׁנֶּאֱמַר: "וְהִגַּדְתָּ לְבִנְךָ בַּיּוֹם הַהוּא לֵאמֹר: בַּעֲבוּר זֶה עָשָׂה יְיָ לִי בְּצֵאתִי מִמִּצְרָיִם". (שמות יג, יח)
"וְהִגַּדְתָּ לְבִנְךָ", יָכוֹל מֵרֹאשׁ חֹדֶשׁ? תַּלְמוּד לוֹמַר: "בַּיּוֹם הַהוּא". אִי "בַּיּוֹם הַהוּא", יָכוֹל מִבְּעוֹד יוֹם? תַּלְמוּד לוֹמַר: "בַּעֲבוּר זֶה", "בַּעֲבוּר זֶה" לֹא אָמַרְתִּי, אֶלָּא בְּשָׁעָה שֶׁיֵּשׁ "מַצָּה" וּ"מָרוֹר" מֻנָּחִים לְפָנֶיךָ.

45

The People of Israel and the Land of Israel

There are people who are comely, but whose dress is repugnant.
And repugnant people, whose dress is comely.
And the People of Israel, whom the Land finds comely and are comely to the Land.

(Bamidbar [Numbers] Raba, XXIII, 5)

The Land of Israel and the People of Israel

This land, which will fall to you as an inheritance (Numbers XXXIV, 2). It is worthy of you.
For example, like a king who owns both male and female servants and marries his male
servants to females belonging to another family. The king stopped and thought and then said:
The male servants are mine and the females are mind. It would be better for me to marry my
male to my female, mine to mine.
Thus, as it were, said the Holy One, Blessed Be He.
The land is Mine, as it is written: The land is the Lord's, and all of its fulness.... (Psalms,
XXIV, 1)
And the People of Israel are Mine, as it is written, For the Children of Israel are My servants
It would be better for Me to bestow My land upon My servants, Mine to Mine.

(Bamidbar [Numbers] Raba, XXIII, 11)

IN THE BEGINNING

our fathers were worshippers of strange gods; but now the All-Present has brought us to His service, as it is said: "And Joshua said unto all the people, Thus says the Lord God of Israel, originally your fathers dwelled beyond the River; Terah, the father of Abraham and father of Nahor; and they served other gods.

And I took your father Abraham from beyond the River, and led him throughout all the land of Canaan, and multiplied his seed, and gave him Isaac. And I gave unto Isaac, Jacob and Esau; and I gave unto Esau, Mount Seir, to possess it; and Jacob and his children went down into Egypt.

מִתְּחִלָּה

עוֹבְדֵי עֲבוֹדָה זָרָה הָיוּ אֲבוֹתֵינוּ, וְעַכְשָׁו קֵרְבָנוּ הַמָּקוֹם לַעֲבוֹדָתוֹ, שֶׁנֶּאֱמַר: "וַיֹּאמֶר יְהוֹשֻׁעַ אֶל כָּל הָעָם: כֹּה אָמַר יְיָ אֱלֹהֵי יִשְׂרָאֵל: בְּעֵבֶר הַנָּהָר יָשְׁבוּ אֲבוֹתֵיכֶם מֵעוֹלָם, תֶּרַח אֲבִי אַבְרָהָם וַאֲבִי נָחוֹר, וַיַּעַבְדוּ אֱלֹהִים אֲחֵרִים. וָאֶקַּח אֶת אֲבִיכֶם, אֶת אַבְרָהָם, מֵעֵבֶר הַנָּהָר, וָאוֹלֵךְ אוֹתוֹ בְּכָל אֶרֶץ כְּנַעַן, וָאַרְבֶּה אֶת זַרְעוֹ, וָאֶתֶּן לוֹ אֶת יִצְחָק, וָאֶתֵּן לְיִצְחָק אֶת יַעֲקֹב וְאֶת עֵשָׂו, וָאֶתֵּן לְעֵשָׂו אֶת הַר שֵׂעִיר, לָרֶשֶׁת אוֹתוֹ, וְיַעֲקֹב וּבָנָיו יָרְדוּ מִצְרָיִם".

47

The Land of Israel was Created for the People of Israel

The Holy One, Blessed Be He took the measure of all of the peoples and could not find a people worthy of receiving the Torah, other than the Desert Generation (the Children of Israel who departed from Egypt).

The Holy One, Blessed Be He took the measure of all the mountains and could not find a mountain on which the Torah should be given, other than Mt. Sinai.

The Holy One, Blessed Be He took the measure of all the cities and could not find a city in which His Temple should be built, other than Jerusalem.

The Holy One, Blessed Be He took the measure of all the lands, and could not find a land worthy of being given to the People of Israel, other than the Land of Israel.

(Vayikrah [Leviticus] Raba XIII, 2)

Blessed be He who keeps His promise to Israel

blessed be He! For the Holy One, blessed be He, designed the end of the bondage in order to fulfill the promise which He had said to Abraham our father in the Covenant between the Portions, as it is said: "And He said unto Abram, know of a certainty that your seed will be a stranger in a land that is not theirs, and shall serve them. And they will afflict them for four hundred years; and also that nation whom they shall serve I will judge; and afterward they shall come out with great riches" *(Gen. 15:13).*

The head of the household covers the Matzot and all take their cup in hand and say

AND IT IS THIS FAITHFULNESS THAT HAS STOOD

by our fathers and us. For not one man only has risen up against us to destroy us, but in every generation men rise up against us to destroy us; but the Holy One, blessed be He, delivers us from their hands.

בָּרוּךְ שׁוֹמֵר הַבְטָחָתוֹ לְיִשְׂרָאֵל, בָּרוּךְ הוּא,

שֶׁהַקָּדוֹשׁ בָּרוּךְ הוּא חִשַּׁב אֶת הַקֵּץ, לַעֲשׂוֹת כְּמָה שֶׁאָמַר לְאַבְרָהָם אָבִינוּ בִּבְרִית בֵּין הַבְּתָרִים, שֶׁנֶּאֱמַר: "וַיֹּאמֶר לְאַבְרָם, יָדוֹעַ תֵּדַע, כִּי גֵר יִהְיֶה זַרְעֲךָ בְּאֶרֶץ לֹא לָהֶם, וַעֲבָדוּם וְעִנּוּ אֹתָם אַרְבַּע מֵאוֹת שָׁנָה, וְגַם אֶת הַגּוֹי אֲשֶׁר יַעֲבֹדוּ דָּן אָנֹכִי, וְאַחֲרֵי כֵן יֵצְאוּ בִּרְכֻשׁ גָּדוֹל". (בְּרֵאשִׁית טו, יג-יד)

מְכַסִּים אֶת הַמַּצּוֹת, מַגְבִּיהִים אֶת הַכּוֹס וְאוֹמְרִים:

וְהִיא שֶׁעָמְדָה לַאֲבוֹתֵינוּ וְלָנוּ, שֶׁלֹּא אֶחָד בִּלְבָד עָמַד עָלֵינוּ לְכַלּוֹתֵנוּ, אֶלָּא שֶׁבְּכָל דּוֹר וָדוֹר עוֹמְדִים עָלֵינוּ לְכַלּוֹתֵנוּ, וְהַקָּדוֹשׁ בָּרוּךְ הוּא מַצִּילֵנוּ מִיָּדָם.

Honey in the Land of Israel

Rabbi Hanina said:
When I came up [to the land of Israel] from the Diaspora, I found a piece of carob and cut it open, and both my hands were streaked with honey.

(Jerusalem Talmud, Pe'ah, LXXXVII, Halacha C)

The Land of Israel – A Land of Values

At the time when Abraham was wandering about Aram Nahara'im and Aram Nachor, he saw the local residents eating and drinking and behaving in a light-headed manner. He said:
Would that I have no share in this land.
When he arrived at Tyre he saw the local residents busy at weeding when it was time to weed and hoeing when it was time to hoe. He said: Would that I have a share in this land.
The Holy One, Blessed Be He said to him: I have given this land to your descendants....
(Genesis XV, 18)

(Braishith [Genesis] Raba XXXIX, 10)

All put their cups down and then the Mazot are uncovered.

COME AND LEARN

what Laban the Aramean sought to do to Jacob our Father. For Pharaoh issued his edict only against the males, but Laban sought to uproot all, as it is said: "An Aramean would have destroyed my Father, and he went down to Egypt and sojourned there, few in number; and he became there a nation, great, mighty and populous" *(Deut. 26:5)*.

"AND HE WENT DOWN INTO EGYPT"...

compelled by the divine decree.

"And sojourned there" – teaching that he did not go to settle, but to sojourn for a time, as it is said, "They said unto Pharaoh, For to sojourn in the land have we come, for your servants have no pasture for their flocks, for the famine is severe in the land of Canaan; now we pray you, let your servants dwell in the land of Goshen". *(Gen. 47:4)*.

מַעֲמִידִים אֶת הַכּוֹס וּמְגַלִּים אֶת הַמַּצּוֹת.

צֵא וּלְמַד

מַה בִּקֵּשׁ לָבָן הָאֲרַמִּי לַעֲשׂוֹת לְיַעֲקֹב אָבִינוּ, שֶׁפַּרְעֹה לֹא גָזַר אֶלָּא עַל הַזְּכָרִים, וְלָבָן בִּקֵּשׁ לַעֲקֹר אֶת הַכֹּל, שֶׁנֶּאֱמַר: "אֲרַמִּי אֹבֵד אָבִי, וַיֵּרֶד מִצְרַיְמָה וַיָּגָר שָׁם בִּמְתֵי מְעָט, וַיְהִי שָׁם לְגוֹי גָּדוֹל, עָצוּם וָרָב". (דְּבָרִים כ, ה-ז)

"וַיֵּרֶד מִצְרַיְמָה"

– אָנוּס עַל פִּי הַדִּבּוּר.

"וַיָּגָר שָׁם" – מְלַמֵּד שֶׁלֹּא יָרַד יַעֲקֹב אָבִינוּ לְהִשְׁתַּקֵּעַ בְּמִצְרַיִם אֶלָּא לָגוּר שָׁם, שֶׁנֶּאֱמַר: "וַיֹּאמְרוּ אֶל פַּרְעֹה: לָגוּר בָּאָרֶץ בָּאנוּ, כִּי אֵין מִרְעֶה לַצֹּאן אֲשֶׁר לַעֲבָדֶיךָ, כִּי כָבֵד הָרָעָב בְּאֶרֶץ כְּנָעַן וְעַתָּה יֵשְׁבוּ נָא עֲבָדֶיךָ בְּאֶרֶץ גֹּשֶׁן". (בְּרֵאשִׁית מז, ד)

The Land of Israel —
A Home for the People of Israel

And God said to Jacob, return to the land of your fathers, to and I will be with you. (Genesis, XXXI, 3) The Holy One, your homeland, Blessed Be He said [to Jacob]: You said, my portion is in the land of the living; return to the land of your fathers.
You father is awaiting you.
Your mother is awaiting you.
I Myself am awaiting you.
And it is written:
There is no blessing in property outside the Land of Israel. Only when you return to the land of your fathers, will I be with you.

(Braishith [Genesis] Raba LXXIV, A)

"Few in number," as it is said: "Your fathers went down into Egypt with seventy persons; and now the Lord thy God has made you as the stars of heaven for multitude" *(Deut. 10:22)*.

"And he became there a nation" – teaching that Israel became a distinct nation there.

"Great, mighty" – as it is said: "And the children of Israel were fruitful, and increased abundantly and multiplied, and waxed exceedingly mighty; and the land was filled with them" *(Ex. 1:7)*.

"And populous," as it is said: "I caused you to multiply as the growth of the field, and you increased and grew up, and you attained excellent beauty; your breasts were fashioned, and your hair was grown; yet you were naked and bare" *(Ezek. 16:7)*.

"בִּמְתֵי מְעָט"

– כְּמָה שֶׁנֶּאֱמַר: "בְּשִׁבְעִים נֶפֶשׁ יָרְדוּ אֲבֹתֶיךָ מִצְרַיְמָה, וְעַתָּה שָׂמְךָ יְיָ אֱלֹהֶיךָ כְּכוֹכְבֵי הַשָּׁמַיִם לָרֹב". (דְּבָרִים י, כב)

"וַיְהִי שָׁם לְגוֹי גָּדוֹל" – מְלַמֵּד שֶׁהָיוּ יִשְׂרָאֵל מְצֻיָּנִים שָׁם.

"עָצוּם" – כְּמָה שֶׁנֶּאֱמַר: "וּבְנֵי יִשְׂרָאֵל פָּרוּ וַיִּשְׁרְצוּ, וַיִּרְבּוּ, וַיַּעַצְמוּ בִּמְאֹד מְאֹד, וַתִּמָּלֵא הָאָרֶץ אֹתָם". (שְׁמוֹת א, ז)

"וָרָב"

– כְּמָה שֶׁנֶּאֱמַר: "רְבָבָה כְּצֶמַח הַשָּׂדֶה נְתַתִּיךְ, וַתִּרְבִּי וַתִּגְדְּלִי, וַתָּבֹאִי בַּעֲדִי עֲדָיִים, שָׁדַיִם נָכֹנוּ, וּשְׂעָרֵךְ צִמֵּחַ, וְאַתְּ עֵרֹם וְעֶרְיָה;
וָאֶעֱבֹר עָלַיִךְ וָאֶרְאֵךְ מִתְבּוֹסֶסֶת בְּדָמָיִךְ, וָאֹמַר לָךְ:
בְּדָמַיִךְ חֲיִי, וָאֹמַר לָךְ: בְּדָמַיִךְ חֲיִי!" (יְחֶזְקֵאל טז, ז)
וַיָּרֵעוּ אֹתָנוּ הַמִּצְרִים וַיְעַנּוּנוּ, וַיִּתְּנוּ עָלֵינוּ עֲבֹדָה קָשָׁה.

The Land of Israel —
A Home for the People of Israel

And God said to Jacob, return to the land of your fathers, to
and I will be with you. (Genesis, XXXI, 3) The Holy One, your
homeland, Blessed Be He said [to Jacob]: You said, my portion
is in the land of the living; return to the land of your fathers.
You father is awaiting you.
Your mother is awaiting you.
I Myself am awaiting you.
And it is written:
There is no blessing in property outside the Land of Israel. Only
when you return to the land of your fathers, will I be with you.

(Braishith [Genesis] Raba LXXIV, A)

"AND THE EGYPTIANS TREATED US WICKEDLY

and afflicted us, and laid upon us hard bondage" *(Deut. 26:6).*

"And the Egyptians treated us wickedly," as it is said, "Come, let us deal wisely with them; lest they multiply, and it come to pass, that when there comes any war, they will join themselves with our enemies, and fight against us, and leave the land" *(Ex. 1:10).*

"And afflicted us," as it is said, "Therefore they set over them taskmasters to afflict them with their burdens. And they built for Pharaoh treasure cities, Pithom and Ramses" *(Ex. 1:11).*

"And laid upon us hard bondage," as it is said: "And the Egyptians made the children of Israel serve with rigor" *(Ex. 1:13).*

"And we cried unto the Lord the God of our fathers and the Lord heard our voice and saw our affliction and our toil and our oppression" *(Deut. 26:7).*
"AND WE CRIED unto the Lord the God of our fathers," as it is said: "And it came to pass in the course of those many days, that the king of Egypt died; and the children of Israel sighed because of their bondage, and they cried, and their cry came unto God because of their bondage" *(Ex. 2:23).*

"וַיָּרֵעוּ אֹתָנוּ הַמִּצְרִים" – כְּמָה שֶׁנֶּאֱמַר: "הָבָה נִתְחַכְּמָה לוֹ, פֶּן יִרְבֶּה, וְהָיָה כִּי תִקְרֶאנָה מִלְחָמָה, וְנוֹסַף גַּם הוּא עַל שֹׂנְאֵינוּ וְנִלְחַם בָּנוּ וְעָלָה מִן הָאָרֶץ". (שמות א, יא)

"וַיְעַנּוּנוּ" – כְּמָה שֶׁנֶּאֱמַר: "וַיָּשִׂימוּ עָלָיו שָׂרֵי מִסִּים לְמַעַן עַנֹּתוֹ בְּסִבְלֹתָם וַיִּבֶן עָרֵי מִסְכְּנוֹת לְפַרְעֹה, אֶת פִּתֹם וְאֶת רַעַמְסֵס". (שמות א, יא)

"וַיִּתְּנוּ עָלֵינוּ עֲבֹדָה קָשָׁה" – כְּמָה שֶׁנֶּאֱמַר: "וַיַּעֲבִדוּ מִצְרַיִם אֶת בְּנֵי יִשְׂרָאֵל בְּפָרֶךְ". (שמות א, יג)

וַנִּצְעַק אֶל יְיָ אֱלֹהֵי אֲבֹתֵינוּ, וַיִּשְׁמַע יְיָ אֶת קֹלֵנוּ, וַיַּרְא אֶת עָנְיֵנוּ וְאֶת עֲמָלֵנוּ וְאֶת לַחֲצֵנוּ.

"וַנִּצְעַק אֶל יְיָ אֱלֹהֵי אֲבֹתֵינוּ"

– כְּמָה שֶׁנֶּאֱמַר: "וַיְהִי בַיָּמִים הָרַבִּים הָהֵם וַיָּמָת מֶלֶךְ מִצְרַיִם, וַיֵּאָנְחוּ בְנֵי יִשְׂרָאֵל מִן הָעֲבֹדָה, וַיִּזְעָקוּ, וַתַּעַל שַׁוְעָתָם אֶל הָאֱלֹהִים מִן הָעֲבֹדָה". (שמות ב, כג)

The Land of Israel – A Bounteous Land

For the Land to which you are going, to inherit it, is not like the Land of Egypt, from which you have departed, where you sowed your seed and watered the land with your feet, like a garden of vegetables.

And the Land to which you are moving, to inherit it, is a land of hills and valleys, which drinks of the rainfall coming down from the sky.

(Deuteronomy, XI, 10-11)

"And the Lord heard our voice," as it is said: "And God heard their groaning, and God remembered His covenant with Abraham, with Isaac, and with Jacob" *(Ex. 2:24)*.

"AND SAW OUR AFFLICTION":

this refers to the separation of man from wife, as it is said: "And God saw the children of Israel, and God knew" *(Ex. 2:25)*.

"And our toil": this refers to the sons, as it is said: "Every son that is born you shall cast into the river, and every daughter you shall save alive" *(Ex. 1:22)*.

"And our oppression": this refers to its severity, as it is said, "Moreover, I have seen the oppression wherewith the Egyptians oppress them" *(Ex. 3:9)*.

"AND THE LORD BROUGHT US OUT

of Egypt with a mighty hand and with an outstretched arm and with great terror and with signs and with wonders" *(Deut. 26:8)*.

"וַיִּשְׁמַע יְיָ אֶת קֹלֵנוּ"

– כְּמָה שֶׁנֶּאֱמַר: "וַיִּשְׁמַע אֱלֹהִים אֶת נַאֲקָתָם, וַיִּזְכֹּר אֱלֹהִים אֶת בְּרִיתוֹ אֶת אַבְרָהָם, אֶת יִצְחָק, וְאֶת יַעֲקֹב". (שמות ב, כד)

"וַיַּרְא אֶת עָנְיֵנוּ" – זוֹ פְּרִישׁוּת דֶּרֶךְ אֶרֶץ, כְּמָה שֶׁנֶּאֱמַר: "וַיַּרְא אֱלֹהִים אֶת בְּנֵי יִשְׂרָאֵל, וַיֵּדַע אֱלֹהִים". (שמות ב, כה)

"וְאֶת עֲמָלֵנוּ" – אֵלּוּ הַבָּנִים, כְּמָה שֶׁנֶּאֱמַר: "כָּל הַבֵּן הַיִּלּוֹד הַיְאֹרָה תַּשְׁלִיכֻהוּ, וְכָל הַבַּת תְּחַיּוּן". (שמות א, כה)

"וְאֶת לַחֲצֵנוּ" – זֶה הַדֹּחַק, כְּמָה שֶׁנֶּאֱמַר: "וְגַם רָאִיתִי אֶת הַלַּחַץ, אֲשֶׁר מִצְרַיִם לֹחֲצִים אֹתָם". (שמות ג, ט)

וַיּוֹצִיאֵנוּ יְיָ מִמִּצְרַיִם בְּיָד חֲזָקָה וּבִזְרֹעַ נְטוּיָה וּבְמֹרָא גָּדֹל וּבְאֹתוֹת וּבְמֹפְתִים.

The Land of Israel – A Preferential Dwelling Place

David said to the Holy One, Blessed Be He: Creator of the universe., even though I own fine and luxurious buildings outside the Land of Israel and I own nothing more than a threshold in the Land of Israel, I would choose to be a doorkeeper [there].

And someone said: Even if I were to have nothing to eat in the Land of Israel but dried out carob fruit, I would choose to be a doorkeeper [there].

(Midrash Tankhuma to Re'eh, VIII)

"And the Lord brought us out of Egypt" – not by the hand of an angel, and not by the hand of a seraph, and not by the hand of a messenger, but the Holy One, blessed be He, in His glory and in His person, as it is said: "For I will go through the land of Egypt in that night, and I will smite all the first-born in the land of Egypt, both man and beast, and against all the gods of Egypt I will execute judgement; I am the Lord" (Ex. 12:12).

"For I will go through the land of Egypt in that night" – I, not an angel; "and I will smite all the first-born in the land of Egypt" – I, not a seraph; "and against all the gods of Egypt I will execute judgement" – I, not a messenger, "I am the Lord" – I am He, and no other.

"WITH A MIGHTY HAND":

this refers to the blight, as it is said, "Behold, the hand of the Lord is upon your cattle which is in the field, upon the horses, upon the asses, upon the camels, upon the herds, and upon the flocks; there shall be a very grievous blight" (Ex. 9:3).

"AND WITH AN OUTSTRETCHED ARM":

this refers to the sword, as it is said, "And a drawn sword in His|hand outstretched over Jerusalem (I Chron. 21:16).

"AND WITH GREAT TERROR":

this refers to the manifestation of the Divine Presence, as it is said: "Or has God ever sought to take Him a nation from the midst of another nation by trials, by signs, and by wonders, and by war, and by a mighty hand, and by an outstretched arm and by great terrors, according to all that the Lord your God did for you in Egypt before your eyes?" (Deut. 4:34)

"וַיּוֹצִאֵנוּ יְיָ מִמִּצְרַיִם"

– לֹא עַל יְדֵי מַלְאָךּ, וְלֹא עַל יְדֵי שָׂרָף, וְלֹא עַל יְדֵי שָׁלִיחַ, אֶלָּא הַקָּדוֹשׁ בָּרוּךְ הוּא בִּכְבוֹדוֹ וּבְעַצְמוֹ. שֶׁנֶּאֱמַר:
"וְעָבַרְתִּי בְאֶרֶץ מִצְרַיִם בַּלַּיְלָה הַזֶּה וְהִכֵּיתִי כָל בְּכוֹר בְּאֶרֶץ מִצְרַיִם, מֵאָדָם וְעַד בְּהֵמָה, וּבְכָל אֱלֹהֵי מִצְרַיִם אֶעֱשֶׂה שְׁפָטִים, אֲנִי יְיָ".
"וְעָבַרְתִּי בְאֶרֶץ מִצְרַיִם בַּלַּיְלָה הַזֶּה" – אֲנִי וְלֹא מַלְאָךּ,
"וְהִכֵּיתִי כָל בְּכוֹר בְּאֶרֶץ מִצְרַיִם" – אֲנִי וְלֹא שָׂרָף,
"וּבְכָל אֱלֹהֵי מִצְרַיִם אֶעֱשֶׂה שְׁפָטִים" – אֲנִי וְלֹא הַשָּׁלִיחַ,
"אֲנִי יְיָ" – אֲנִי הוּא וְלֹא אַחֵר.

"בְּיָד חֲזָקָה"

– זוֹ הַדֶּבֶר, כְּמָה שֶׁנֶּאֱמַר:
"הִנֵּה יַד יְיָ הוֹיָה בְּמִקְנְךָ אֲשֶׁר בַּשָּׂדֶה,
בַּסּוּסִים, בַּחֲמֹרִים, בַּגְּמַלִּים, בַּבָּקָר וּבַצֹּאן, דֶּבֶר כָּבֵד מְאֹד". (שְׁמוֹת ט, ג)

"וּבִזְרֹעַ נְטוּיָה"

– זוֹ הַחֶרֶב, כְּמָה שֶׁנֶּאֱמַר:
"וְחַרְבּוֹ שְׁלוּפָה בְּיָדוֹ, נְטוּיָה עַל יְרוּשָׁלַםִ". (דִּבְרֵי הַיָּמִים א כא, ט-ז)

"וּבְמֹרָא גָּדֹל"

– זֶה גִּלּוּי שְׁכִינָה, כְּמָה שֶׁנֶּאֱמַר:
"אוֹ הֲנִסָּה אֱלֹהִים לָבוֹא לָקַחַת לוֹ גוֹי מִקֶּרֶב גּוֹי בְּמַסֹּת, בְּאֹתֹת וּבְמוֹפְתִים וּבְמִלְחָמָה וּבְיָד חֲזָקָה וּבִזְרוֹעַ נְטוּיָה וּבְמוֹרָאִים גְּדֹלִים, כְּכֹל אֲשֶׁר עָשָׂה לָכֶם יְיָ אֱלֹהֵיכֶם בְּמִצְרַיִם לְעֵינֶיךָ". (דְּבָרִים ד, לד)

The Land of Israel – Dearer than all Other Lands

Dear is the Land of Israel, which the Holy One, Blessed Be He chose.
You can see that when He created the world He distributed the [other] lands to the Ministers of the other nations, but chose the Land of Israel [for Himself].
How do we know this? Since Moses said: When the Mightest One gave the nations of the world their inheritance.... (Deuteronomy XXXII, 8)
And chose the Land of Israel as His portion, as it is written: For the Lord's portion is His people, Jacob the region of His legacy.

(Deuteronomy, XXXII, 9)

The Holy One, Blessed Be He Said: May the People of Israel come as though they were coming to My portion, and settle the land which has been allotted Me.

(Midrash Tankhuma to Re'eh, VIII)

"AND WITH SIGNS":

this refers to the Rod, as it is said: "Take this rod in your hand, with which you will do all these signs" *(Ex. 4:17)*.

While reciting the words: "blood, and fire, and pillars of smoke," the Ten Plagues, and the three abbreviations that follow, remove a drop of wine from the cup with the little finger at each word.

"AND WITH WONDERS":

this refers to the blood, as it is said: "And I will show wonders in the heavens and in the earth;

When this point in the Seder service is reached, it is the custom to drip three drops of wine from the cup.

BLOOD, AND FIRE, AND PILLARS OF SMOKE" *(Joel 2:30)*.

Another explanation is as follows: "With a strong hand" indicates two plagues; "and with an outstretched arm," two; "and with great terror," two; "and with signs," two; "and with wonders," two.

"וּבְאֹתוֹת"

– זֶה הַמַּטֶּה, כְּמָה שֶׁנֶּאֱמַר: "וְאֶת הַמַּטֶּה הַזֶּה תִּקַּח בְּיָדֶךָ, אֲשֶׁר תַּעֲשֶׂה בּוֹ אֶת הָאֹתֹת". (שמות ד, יז)

"וּבְמֹפְתִים"

– זֶה הַדָּם, כְּמָה שֶׁנֶּאֱמַר: "וְנָתַתִּי מוֹפְתִים בַּשָּׁמַיִם וּבָאָרֶץ". (יואל ג, ג)

כְּשֶׁמַּגִּיעִים לְכָאן נוֹהֲגִים לְטַפְטֵף שָׁלוֹשׁ טִפּוֹת יַיִן מִן הַכּוֹס.

"דָּם וָאֵשׁ וְתִימְרוֹת עָשָׁן".

דָּבָר אַחֵר: "בְּיָד חֲזָקָה" – שְׁתַּיִם, "וּבִזְרֹעַ נְטוּיָה" – שְׁתַּיִם, "וּבְמֹרָא גָּדֹל" – שְׁתַּיִם, "וּבְאֹתוֹת" – שְׁתַּיִם, "וּבְמֹפְתִים" – שְׁתַּיִם.

אֵלוּ עֶשֶׂר מַכּוֹת, שֶׁהֵבִיא הַקָּדוֹשׁ בָּרוּךְ הוּא עַל הַמִּצְרִים בְּמִצְרַים, וְאֵלוּ הֵן:

כְּשֶׁמַּזְכִּירִים אֶת הַמַּכּוֹת נוֹהֲגִים לְטַפְטֵף, טִפָּה לְכָל מַכָּה.
אוֹ לִשְׁפֹּךְ יַיִן מִן הַכּוֹס.

דָּם
צְפַרְדֵּעַ
כִּנִּים
עָרוֹב
דֶּבֶר
שְׁחִין
בָּרָד
אַרְבֶּה
חֹשֶׁךְ
מַכַּת בְּכוֹרוֹת

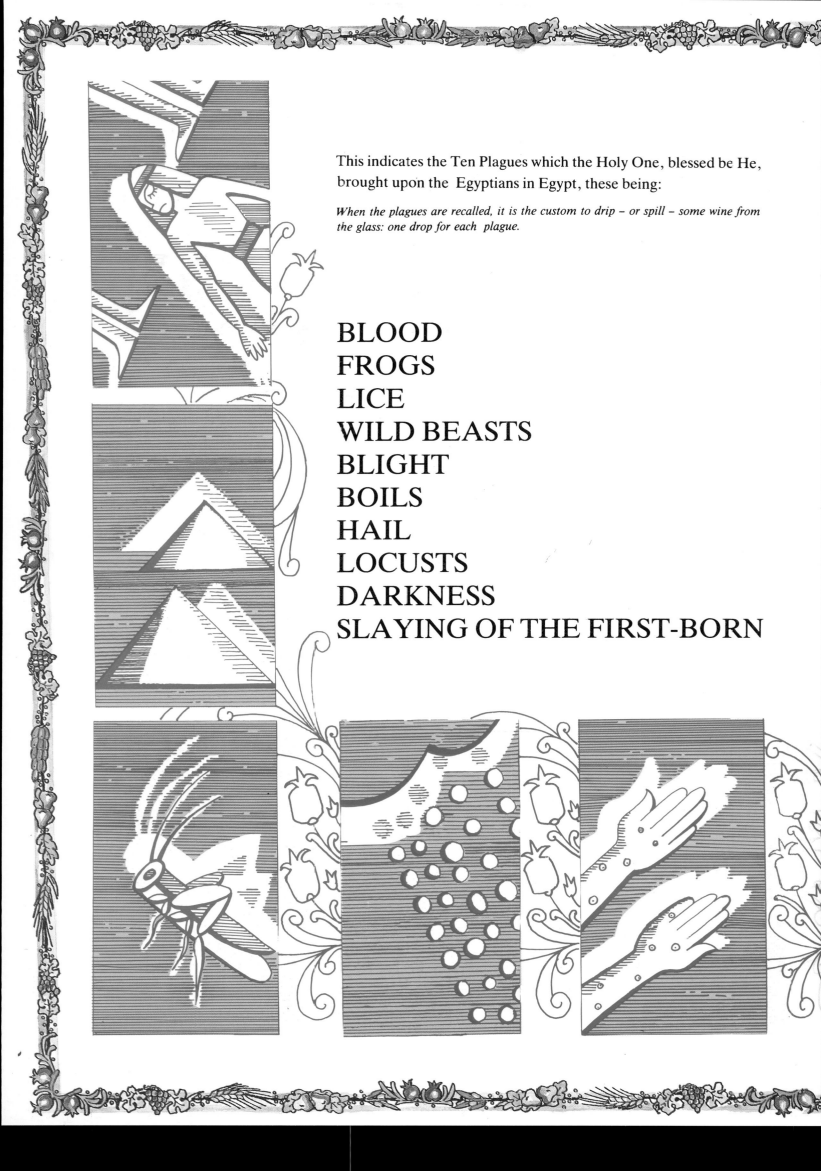

This indicates the Ten Plagues which the Holy One, blessed be He, brought upon the Egyptians in Egypt, these being:

When the plagues are recalled, it is the custom to drip – or spill – some wine from the glass: one drop for each plague.

BLOOD
FROGS
LICE
WILD BEASTS
BLIGHT
BOILS
HAIL
LOCUSTS
DARKNESS
SLAYING OF THE FIRST-BORN

The Land of Israel is More Precious than all Other Lands

A land of which the patriarchs of the world were envious.
Abraham coveted it, for he says:
Lord, God, how will I know that I will inherit it? (Genesis, XV, 8)
Isaac coveted it, as it was said to him:
Dwell in this land, and I will be with you and bless you, for to you and your descendants will I give all these lands. (Genesis XXVI, 3)
Jacob coveted it, as it is written:
If the Lord God be with me ... I will return in peace to my father's house.... (Genesis, XXVIII, 20-21)

Rabbi Judah said: even Moses coveted it, as it is written:
And I will beseech God ... that I will pass over and see.... (Deuteronomy, III, 23-25)
And even David coveted it, as it is written:
Rather would I be doorkeeper in the house of my God.... (Psalms, LXXXIV, 11)

(Midrash Tankhuma to Re'eh, VIII)

Also when the indications are recalled, it is the custom to drip drops of wine from the glass: one drop for each.

Rabbi Judah used to refer to them by abbreviation, thus:

DETSACH   ADASH   BE'AHAB

The glasses are refilled with wine, and the recitation of the hagaddah continues.

Rabbi Jose the Galilean said: "How can you deduce that if the Egyptians were smitten with ten plagues in Egypt, then upon the sea they were smitten with fifty? With regard to

Egypt, what does the text say? 'Then the magicians said unto Pharaoh, This is the finger of God' *(Ex. 8:15)*; and at the sea, what does the text say? 'And Israel saw the great hand which the Lord laid upon the Egyptians; and the people feared the Lord, and they believed in the Lord, and in His servant Moses' *(Ex. 14:31)*. How many were they smitten by the finger? Ten plagues. Deduce hence that in Egypt they were smitten with ten plagues, while at the sea they were smitten with fifty plagues."

רַבִּי יְהוּדָה הָיָה נוֹתֵן בָּהֶם סִימָנִים:

גַּם בְּהַזְכָּרַת הַסִּימָנִים נוֹהֲגִים לְטַפְטֵף טִפּוֹת יַיִן מִן הַכּוֹס. טִפָּה לְכָל סִימָן.

דְּצַ"ךְ עַדַ"שׁ בְּאַחַ"ב.

מְמַלְּאִים אֶת הַכּוֹסוֹת בְּיַיִן מֵחָדָשׁ, וּמַמְשִׁיכִים לִקְרֹא בַּהַגָּדָה.

רַבִּי יוֹסֵי הַגְּלִילִי אוֹמֵר:

מִנַּיִן אַתָּה אוֹמֵר, שֶׁלָּקוּ הַמִּצְרִים בְּמִצְרַיִם עֶשֶׂר מַכּוֹת, וְעַל הַיָּם לָקוּ חֲמִשִּׁים מַכּוֹת? בְּמִצְרַיִם מַה הוּא אוֹמֵר? "וַיֹּאמְרוּ הַחַרְטֻמִּם אֶל פַּרְעֹה: אֶצְבַּע אֱלֹהִים הוּא" (שמות ח, טו),

וְעַל הַיָּם מַה הוּא אוֹמֵר? "וַיַּרְא יִשְׂרָאֵל אֶת הַיָּד הַגְּדֹלָה, אֲשֶׁר עָשָׂה יְיָ בְּמִצְרַיִם, וַיִּירְאוּ הָעָם אֶת יְיָ, וַיַּאֲמִינוּ בַּיְיָ וּבְמֹשֶׁה עַבְדּוֹ". (שמות יד, לא)

כַּמָּה לָקוּ בְּאֶצְבַּע? עֶשֶׂר מַכּוֹת! אֱמֹר מֵעַתָּה: בְּמִצְרַיִם לָקוּ עֶשֶׂר מַכּוֹת, וְעַל הַיָּם לָקוּ חֲמִשִּׁים מַכּוֹת.

Building the Land of Israel

"Why was Omri worthy of being a king?
Since he added a district to the Land of Israel.
As it is written: He purchased and he fortified
the hill and named the city he had the hill of Samaria
from Shemer for two measures of silver, constructed,
Samaria, after Shemer, the owner of the hill.

(I Kings, XVI, 24)

(Sanhedrin CII, 2B)

Rabbi Eliezer said: "From where may it be deduced that every plague which the Holy One, blessed be He, brought upon the Egyptians in Egypt was equivalent to four plagues? It is said: 'He cast upon them the fierceness of His anger, wrath, and indignation, and trouble, a band of angels of evil' *(Ps. 77:49)*.

'WRATH' indicates one;

'INDIGNATION,' two;

'TRIUBLE,' three;

'A BAND OF ANGELS OF EVIL,' four.

Deduce then that in Egypt they were smitten with forty plagues, while at the sea they were afflicted with two hundred plagues."

Rabbi Akiva said: "From where may it be deduced that every plague which the Holy One, blessed be He, brought upon the Egyptians in Egypt was equivalent to five plagues? It is written: 'He cast upon them the fierceness of His anger, wrath, and indignation, and trouble, a band of angels of evil'.

'THE FIERCENESS OF HIS ANGER' indicates one;

'WRATH,' two;

'INDIGNATION,' three;

'TROUBLE,' four;

'A BAND OF ANGELS OF EVIL,' five.

Deduce then that in Egypt they were smitten with fifty plagues, while at the sea they were smitten with two hundred and fifty plagues."

רַבִּי אֱלִיעֶזֶר אוֹמֵר:

מִנַּיִן שֶׁכָּל מַכָּה וּמַכָּה שֶׁהֵבִיא הַקָּדוֹשׁ בָּרוּךְ הוּא עַל הַמִּצְרִים בְּמִצְרַיִם הָיְתָה שֶׁל אַרְבַּע מַכּוֹת? שֶׁנֶּאֱמַר: "יְשַׁלַּח בָּם חֲרוֹן אַפּוֹ, עֶבְרָה וָזַעַם וְצָרָה, מִשְׁלַחַת מַלְאֲכֵי רָעִים". (תְּהִלִים עח, מט)

"עֶבְרָה" – **אַחַת**, "וָזַעַם" – **שְׁתַּיִם**, "וְצָרָה" – **שָׁלוֹשׁ**, "מִשְׁלַחַת מַלְאֲכֵי רָעִים" – **אַרְבַּע**. אֱמֹר מֵעַתָּה: בְּמִצְרַיִם לָקוּ אַרְבָּעִים מַכּוֹת, וְעַל הַיָּם לָקוּ מָאתַיִם מַכּוֹת.

רַבִּי עֲקִיבָא אוֹמֵר:

מִנַּיִן שֶׁכָּל מַכָּה וּמַכָּה שֶׁהֵבִיא הַקָּדוֹשׁ בָּרוּךְ הוּא עַל הַמִּצְרִים בְּמִצְרַיִם הָיְתָה שֶׁל חָמֵשׁ מַכּוֹת? שֶׁנֶּאֱמַר: "יְשַׁלַּח בָּם חֲרוֹן אַפּוֹ, עֶבְרָה וָזַעַם וְצָרָה, מִשְׁלַחַת מַלְאֲכֵי רָעִים". (שָׁם, שָׁם)

"חֲרוֹן אַפּוֹ" – **אַחַת**, "עֶבְרָה" – **שְׁתַּיִם**, "וָזַעַם" – **שָׁלוֹשׁ**, "וְצָרָה" – **אַרְבַּע**, "מִשְׁלַחַת מַלְאֲכֵי רָעִים" – **חָמֵשׁ**. אֱמֹר מֵעַתָּה: בְּמִצְרַיִם לָקוּ חֲמִשִּׁים מַכּוֹת, וְעַל הַיָּם לָקוּ חֲמִשִּׁים וּמָאתַיִם מַכּוֹת.

כֵּן יִשְׂרָאֵל
מְעַלְלוֹת
טוֹבוֹת
לְמִידִים
עָלֵינוּ

FOR HOW MUCH DO WE OWE THE ALMIGHTY OUR THANKFULNESS!

Had He brought us out of Egypt, and not executed judgement on them –
it would have sufficed us!
Had He executed judgement on them, but not wrought justice on their gods –
it would have sufficed us!
Had He wrought justice on their gods, and not slain their first-born – sufficed us!
Had he slain their first-born, and not given us their riches – it would have sufficed us!
Had He given us their riches, and not split the sea for us – it would have sufficed us!
Had He split the sea for us, and not brought us through it on dry land –
it would have sufficed us!
Had He brought us through it on dry land, and not sunk our oppressors in its depths –
it would have sufficed us!
Had He sunk our oppressors in its depths, and not satisfied our wants in the wilderness
for forty years – it would have sufficed us!
Had He satisfied our wants in the wilderness for forty years, and not fed us with the
manna – it would have sufficed us!
Had He fed us with the manna, and not given us the Sabbath – it would have sufficed us!
Had He given us the Sabbath, and not brought us to Mount Sinai –
it would have sufficed us!
Had He brought us to Mount Sinai, and not given us the Torah –
it would have sufficed us!
Had He given us the Torah, and not brought us into the Land of Israel –
it would have sufficed us!
Had He brought us into the Land of Israel, and not built us the Temple –
it would have sufficed us!

כַּמָּה מַעֲלוֹת טוֹבוֹת לַמָּקוֹם עָלֵינוּ:

אִלּוּ הוֹצִיאָנוּ מִמִּצְרַיִם וְלֹא עָשָׂה בָהֶם שְׁפָטִים,‎ דַּיֵּנוּ.
אִלּוּ עָשָׂה בָהֶם שְׁפָטִים וְלֹא עָשָׂה בֵאלֹהֵיהֶם,‎ דַּיֵּנוּ.
אִלּוּ עָשָׂה בֵאלֹהֵיהֶם וְלֹא הָרַג אֶת בְּכוֹרֵיהֶם,‎ דַּיֵּנוּ.
אִלּוּ הָרַג אֶת בְּכוֹרֵיהֶם וְלֹא נָתַן לָנוּ אֶת מָמוֹנָם,‎ דַּיֵּנוּ.
אִלּוּ נָתַן לָנוּ אֶת מָמוֹנָם וְלֹא קָרַע לָנוּ אֶת הַיָּם,‎ דַּיֵּנוּ.
אִלּוּ קָרַע לָנוּ אֶת הַיָּם וְלֹא הֶעֱבִירָנוּ בְתוֹכוֹ בֶּחָרָבָה,‎ דַּיֵּנוּ.
אִלּוּ הֶעֱבִירָנוּ בְתוֹכוֹ בֶּחָרָבָה וְלֹא שִׁקַּע צָרֵינוּ בְּתוֹכוֹ,‎ דַּיֵּנוּ.
אִלּוּ שִׁקַּע צָרֵינוּ בְּתוֹכוֹ וְלֹא סִפֵּק צָרְכֵּנוּ בַּמִּדְבָּר אַרְבָּעִים שָׁנָה,‎ דַּיֵּנוּ.
אִלּוּ סִפֵּק צָרְכֵּנוּ בַּמִּדְבָּר אַרְבָּעִים שָׁנָה וְלֹא הֶאֱכִילָנוּ אֶת הַמָּן,‎ דַּיֵּנוּ.
אִלּוּ הֶאֱכִילָנוּ אֶת הַמָּן וְלֹא נָתַן לָנוּ אֶת הַשַּׁבָּת,‎ דַּיֵּנוּ.
אִלּוּ נָתַן לָנוּ אֶת הַשַּׁבָּת וְלֹא קֵרְבָנוּ לִפְנֵי הַר סִינַי,‎ דַּיֵּנוּ.
אִלּוּ קֵרְבָנוּ לִפְנֵי הַר סִינַי וְלֹא נָתַן לָנוּ אֶת הַתּוֹרָה,‎ דַּיֵּנוּ.
אִלּוּ נָתַן לָנוּ אֶת הַתּוֹרָה וְלֹא הִכְנִיסָנוּ לְאֶרֶץ יִשְׂרָאֵל,‎ דַּיֵּנוּ.
אִלּוּ הִכְנִיסָנוּ לְאֶרֶץ יִשְׂרָאֵל וְלֹא בָנָה לָנוּ אֶת בֵּית הַבְּחִירָה,‎ דַּיֵּנוּ.

The Names of Places in the Land of Israel

Hammat is Tiberias, yet why is it called Hammat? On account of Hamei Tiberias [the Tiberias Hot Springs].

Ra'akath is Zippori, yet why is it called Ra'akath? Since like a river bank ["rakta" in Aramaic] it elevated above its surroundings.

Kinnereth is Ginnosar, yet why is it called Kinnereth? Since its fruits are as sweet as the sound of a violin ["kinrei" in Aramaic].

And why is the city of Tiberias so called? Since it is located in the navel ["tabur," in Hebrew] of the Land of Israel.

Kitron is Zippori. And why is it called Zippori? Since it is located on the crest of a mountain, like a bird ["tzipor," in Hebrew].

(Megillah VI, B)

HOW MUCH MORE SO,

then, must we be thankful to the all-Present! For He brought us out of Egypt, and executed judgement on them, and wrought justice on their gods, and slew their first-born, and gave us their substance, and split the sea for us, and brought us through it on dry land, and sank our oppressors in its depths, and satisfied our wants in the wilderness for forty years, and fed us with the manna, and gave us the Sabbath, and brought us to Mount Sinai, and gave us the Torah, and brought us into the land of Israel and built us the Temple to atone for all our sins.

עַל אַחַת כַּמָּה וְכַמָּה, טוֹבָה כְפוּלָה וּמְכֻפֶּלֶת לַמָּקוֹם עָלֵינוּ:

שֶׁהוֹצִיאָנוּ מִמִּצְרַיִם, וְעָשָׂה בָהֶם שְׁפָטִים, וְעָשָׂה בֵאלֹהֵיהֶם, וְהָרַג אֶת בְּכוֹרֵיהֶם, וְנָתַן לָנוּ אֶת מָמוֹנָם, וְקָרַע לָנוּ אֶת הַיָּם, וְהֶעֱבִירָנוּ בְתוֹכוֹ בֶּחָרָבָה, וְשִׁקַּע צָרֵינוּ בְּתוֹכוֹ, וְסִפֵּק צָרְכֵּנוּ בַּמִּדְבָּר אַרְבָּעִים שָׁנָה, וְהֶאֱכִילָנוּ אֶת הַמָּן, וְנָתַן לָנוּ אֶת הַשַּׁבָּת, וְקֵרְבָנוּ לִפְנֵי הַר סִינַי, וְנָתַן לָנוּ אֶת הַתּוֹרָה, וְהִכְנִיסָנוּ לְאֶרֶץ יִשְׂרָאֵל, וּבָנָה לָנוּ אֶת בֵּית הַבְּחִירָה לְכַפֵּר עַל כָּל עֲוֹנוֹתֵינוּ.

לְאֶרֶץ יִשְׂרָאֵל

The People of Israel are One People

The People of Israel are compared to a lamb.
Rabbi Hizkiah taught: Why are the People of Israel compared to a lamb? When a lamb sustains an injury to its head or one of its organs, the pain is felt in all of its organs, so it is with the People of Israel; when one of them sins, all the others feel it.
Rabbi Shimon ben Yochai said: A comparison can be made with people who sit in a boat and one of them takes a drill and start drilling a hole under him.
The others said to him: What do you think you're doing?
He replied: What concern is it of yours; I'm only drilling here, where I'm sitting.
They said to him: [It is our concern], since the water will come in and flood the entire ship.

(Vayikra [Leviticus] Raba IV, 6)

Rabban Gamliel said: "Any person who does not make mention of the following three things on Passover has not fulfilled his obligation; and these are they:

THE PASCHAL LAMB, MATZAH, BITTER HERBS."

The shank bone which is on the Passover plate is pointed to, and the following is recited:

THE PASCHAL LAMB

which our fathers used to eat at the time when the Temple was standing – what was the reason? It is because the Holy One, Blessed be He, passed over the houses of our fathers in Egypt, as it is said: "And you shall say, It is the sacrifice of the Lord's Passover, for he passed over the houses of the children of Israel in Egypt when he smote the Egyptians, and safeguarded our houses. And the people bowed their heads, and worshipped" (Ex. 12:27).

רַבָּן גַּמְלִיאֵל הָיָה אוֹמֵר:

כָּל שֶׁלֹּא אָמַר שְׁלוֹשָׁה דְבָרִים אֵלּוּ בַּפֶּסַח, לֹא יָצָא יְדֵי חוֹבָתוֹ, וְאֵלּוּ הֵן: פֶּסַח, מַצָּה וּמָרוֹר

מַרְאִים עַל הַזְּרוֹעַ הַמֻּנַחַת בַּקְּעָרָה וְאוֹמְרִים:

פֶּסַח

שֶׁהָיוּ אֲבוֹתֵינוּ אוֹכְלִים, בִּזְמַן שֶׁבֵּית הַמִּקְדָּשׁ הָיָה קַיָּם, עַל שׁוּם מָה?

עַל שׁוּם שֶׁפָּסַח הַקָּדוֹשׁ בָּרוּךְ הוּא עַל בָּתֵּי אֲבוֹתֵינוּ בְּמִצְרַיִם, שֶׁנֶּאֱמַר: "וַאֲמַרְתֶּם זֶבַח פֶּסַח הוּא לַיָי, אֲשֶׁר פָּסַח עַל בָּתֵּי בְּנֵי יִשְׂרָאֵל בְּמִצְרַיִם, בְּנָגְפּוֹ אֶת מִצְרַיִם, וְאֶת בָּתֵּינוּ הִצִּיל; וַיִּקֹּד הָעָם וַיִּשְׁתַּחֲוּוּ". (שמות יב, כז)

מַנִּיחִים אֶת הַזְּרוֹעַ בִּמְקוֹמָהּ עַל קְעָרַת הַסֵּדֶר.

Hopes for Redemption

And so, that which is written, The land will be turned into a wasteland by your enemies (Leviticus XXVI, 32) is good news which is proclaimed for all the periods of exile. For our land does not welcome our enemies. And this too is great proof and a promise that throughout the world no land can be found which is so good and spacious and which was once settled and yet remains in ruin, like the Land of Israel. For from the time that we left it, no people or nation has received it, and all of them have attempted to settle it, and they cannot attain this.

(According to the Exegesis of the Ramban [Nachmanides] to Leviticus, XXVI, 16)

The matzot are lifted up and shown to everyone, and the following is recited:

THIS MATZAH

which we eat – what is the reason? It is because there was not time for the dough of our fathers to become leavened before the supreme King of Kings, the Holy One, Blessed be He, revealed himself unto them and redeemed them, as it is said: "And they baked unleavened cakes of the dough which they brought forth out of Egypt, for it was not leavened; because they were thrust out of Egypt, and could not tarry, neither had they prepared for themselves any provisions" *(Ex. 12:39)*.

The matzot are returned to the Passover plate.
The bitter herbs which are on the Passover plate are pointed to, and the following is recited:

THIS BITTER HERB

which we eat – What is the reason? It is because the Egyptians embittered the lives of our fathers in Egypt, as it is written: "And they made their lives bitter with hard bondage, in mortar and in bricks, and in all types of work in the field; all their work which they made them perform was with rigor" *(Ex. 1:14)*.

IN EVERY GENERATION IT IS EACH ONE'S DUTY TO REGARD HIMSELF AS IF HE HAD GONE FORTH FROM EGYPT,

מַגְבִּיהִים אֶת הַמַּצָּה, מַרְאִים אוֹתָהּ לְכָל הַמְסֻבִּים וְאוֹמְרִים:

מַצָּה

זוֹ, שֶׁאָנוּ אוֹכְלִים, עַל שׁוּם מָה?

עַל שׁוּם שֶׁלֹּא הִסְפִּיק בְּצֵקָם שֶׁל אֲבוֹתֵינוּ לְהַחֲמִיץ, עַד שֶׁנִּגְלָה עֲלֵיהֶם מֶלֶךְ מַלְכֵי הַמְּלָכִים, הַקָּדוֹשׁ בָּרוּךְ הוּא וּגְאָלָם, שֶׁנֶּאֱמַר: "וַיֹּאפוּ אֶת הַבָּצֵק, אֲשֶׁר הוֹצִיאוּ מִמִּצְרַיִם עֻגֹת מַצּוֹת, כִּי לֹא חָמֵץ; כִּי גֹרְשׁוּ מִמִּצְרַיִם וְלֹא יָכְלוּ לְהִתְמַהְמֵהַּ, וְגַם צֵדָה לֹא עָשׂוּ לָהֶם". (שְׁמוֹת יב, לט)

מַנִּיחִים אֶת הַמַּצָּה בִּמְקוֹמָהּ עַל קַעֲרַת הַסֵּדֶר.

מַרְאִים לְכָל הַמְסֻבִּים אֶת הַמָּרוֹר הַמֻּנָּח עַל הַקְּעָרָה וְאוֹמְרִים:

מָרוֹר

זֶה, שֶׁאָנוּ אוֹכְלִים, עַל שׁוּם מָה? עַל שׁוּם שֶׁמֵּרְרוּ הַמִּצְרִים אֶת חַיֵּי אֲבוֹתֵינוּ בְּמִצְרַיִם, שֶׁנֶּאֱמַר: "וַיְמָרְרוּ אֶת חַיֵּיהֶם בַּעֲבֹדָה קָשָׁה, בְּחֹמֶר וּבִלְבֵנִים, וּבְכָל עֲבֹדָה בַּשָּׂדֶה, אֵת כָּל עֲבֹדָתָם, אֲשֶׁר עָבְדוּ בָהֶם בְּפָרֶךְ". (שְׁמוֹת א, יד)

בְּכָל דּוֹר וָדוֹר

מַנִּיחִים אֶת הַמָּרוֹר בִּמְקוֹמוֹ עַל קַעֲרַת הַסֵּדֶר.

בְּכָל דּוֹר וָדוֹר חַיָּב אָדָם לִרְאוֹת אֶת עַצְמוֹ כְּאִלּוּ הוּא יָצָא מִמִּצְרַיִם.

The Land of Israel — Its Size and its Breadth

It is written in the Book of Deuteronomy, chapter 12, verse 20: When the Lord your God enlarges your territory, as He has told you....

The sages asked: Can it be possible that the Holy One, Blessed Be He will expand the Land of Israel?

Rabbi Yitzhak said: The Land of Israel is like a scroll. When it is rolled up there is no way of knowing what its length is and what is its width. When it is unrolled, it proclaims what it is. So it is with the Land of Israel, which is, for the most part, hills and mountains. As it is written in the Torah:

And the land to which you are moving, to inherit it, is a land of hills and valleys, which drinks of the rainfall coming down from the sky. A land which the Lord your God keeps watch over; the eyes of the Lord your God are on it always, from the first day of the new year, until the last. (Deuteronomy XI, 11-12)

When the Holy One, Blessed Be He straightens it, then the land will proclaim what it truly is.

(Dvarim [Deuteronomy] Raba, IV, 10)

IN EVERY GENERATION IT IS EACH ONE'S DUTY TO REGARD HIMSELF AS IF HE HAD GONE FORTH FROM EGYPT,

as it is written: "And you shall tell your son in that day, saying, Because of that which the Lord did for me when I came forth out of Egypt" *(Ex 13:8)*. It was not only our fathers that the Holy One, Blessed be He, redeemed, but us too He redeemed with them; as it is said: "And He brought us out from there, so that He might bring us in, to give us the land which He swore unto your fathers" *(Deut 6:23)*.

The matzot are covered, the glass of wine is lifted up and the following is recited in a loud voice:

IT IS THEREFORE OUR DUTY

to thank, praise, laud, glorify, exalt, honor, bless, extol, and adore Him who performed all these wonders for our fathers and for us. He brought us forth from slavery to freedom, from anguish to joy, from mourning to a holy day, from darkness to great light, and from bondage to redemption.

LET US THEREFORE SING BEFORE HIM A NEW SONG, HALLELUYAH!

The glass is put down and the matzot are uncovered.

Psalm 113: HALLELUYAH! Praise, you servants of the Lord, praise the Name of the Lord. Let the Name of the Lord be blessed from this time forth and for evermore. From the rising of the sun until its going down the Lord's Name is to be praised. The Lord is high above all nations, and His glory above the heavens. Who is like unto the Lord our God, that dwells so high; that looks down so low upon the heavens and earth! He raised up the lowly out of the dust, and lifts up the needy from the dunghill;

to set him with princes, with the princes of His people. He makes the barren woman dwell in her house as a joyful mother of children. Halleluyah!

שֶׁנֶּאֱמַר: "וְהִגַּדְתָּ לְבִנְךָ בַּיּוֹם הַהוּא לֵאמֹר: בַּעֲבוּר זֶה עָשָׂה יְיָ לִי, בְּצֵאתִי מִמִּצְרָיִם". (שְׁמוֹת יג, ח)
לֹא אֶת אֲבוֹתֵינוּ בִּלְבַד גָּאַל הַקָּדוֹשׁ בָּרוּךְ הוּא, אֶלָּא אַף אוֹתָנוּ גָּאַל עִמָּהֶם, שֶׁנֶּאֱמַר: "וְאוֹתָנוּ הוֹצִיא מִשָּׁם לְמַעַן הָבִיא אֹתָנוּ לָתֶת לָנוּ אֶת הָאָרֶץ, אֲשֶׁר נִשְׁבַּע לַאֲבֹתֵינוּ". (דְּבָרִים ו, כג)

מְכַסִּים אֶת הַמַּצּוֹת, מַגְבִּיהִים אֶת כּוֹס הַיַּיִן וְאוֹמְרִים בְּקוֹל רָם:

לְפִיכָךְ

אֲנַחְנוּ חַיָּבִים לְהוֹדוֹת, לְהַלֵּל, לְשַׁבֵּחַ, לְפָאֵר, לְרוֹמֵם, לְהַדֵּר, לְבָרֵךְ, לְעַלֵּה וּלְקַלֵּס לְמִי שֶׁעָשָׂה לַאֲבוֹתֵינוּ וְלָנוּ אֶת כָּל הַנִּסִּים הָאֵלֶּה: הוֹצִיאָנוּ מֵעַבְדוּת לְחֵרוּת, מִיָּגוֹן לְשִׂמְחָה, מֵאֵבֶל לְיוֹם טוֹב, וּמֵאֲפֵלָה לְאוֹר גָּדוֹל וּמִשִּׁעְבּוּד לִגְאֻלָּה. וְנֹאמַר לְפָנָיו שִׁירָה חֲדָשָׁה: הַלְלוּיָהּ.

מַעֲמִידִים אֶת הַכּוֹס וּמְגַלִּים אֶת הַמַּצּוֹת.

הַלְלוּיָהּ הַלְלוּ עַבְדֵי יְיָ הַלְלוּ אֶת שֵׁם יְיָ. יְהִי שֵׁם יְיָ מְבֹרָךְ מֵעַתָּה וְעַד עוֹלָם. מִמִּזְרַח שֶׁמֶשׁ עַד מְבוֹאוֹ מְהֻלָּל שֵׁם יְיָ. רָם עַל כָּל גּוֹיִם יְיָ, עַל הַשָּׁמַיִם כְּבוֹדוֹ. מִי כַּיְיָ אֱלֹהֵינוּ, הַמַּגְבִּיהִי לָשָׁבֶת. הַמַּשְׁפִּילִי לִרְאוֹת בַּשָּׁמַיִם וּבָאָרֶץ. מְקִימִי מֵעָפָר דָּל, מֵאַשְׁפֹּת יָרִים אֶבְיוֹן. לְהוֹשִׁיבִי עִם נְדִיבִים, עִם נְדִיבֵי עַמּוֹ. מוֹשִׁיבִי עֲקֶרֶת הַבַּיִת, אֵם הַבָּנִים שְׂמֵחָה, הַלְלוּיָהּ. (תְּהִלִּים קיג)

A Great Love for the Land of Israel

Rabbi Aba used to kiss the rocks and corals of Acre, which was situated at the outermost boundary of the Land of Israel during the time of the Second Temple and afterwards. (The boundary set by those who returned from exile in Babylon)
Rabbi Hanina used to level the uneven places of the Land of Israel, because of his love for the land, which was dear to him, that those who were passing through should not run into any obstacles and then speak badly of the land.

Rabbi Ami and Rabbi Asi used to move from the sun to the shade and from the shade to the sun, so that they would always be seated in comfort and so that no one would be able to say that they were uncomfortable in the Land of Israel.
Rabbi Hiya used to roll in the dust of the Land of Israel, and this act was a hint of sorts that the Land of Israel was not desirable to the sages because of its many qualities, but for the plain love of the land, that even its rocks and dust were important to them.

(According to the Exegesis of Rabbi Adin Steinsaltz to the Talmud: Ketuboth CXII, E)

Psalm 114: **WHEN ISRAEL WENT FORTH OUT OF EGYPT,** the house of
Jacob from the people of a strange language; Judah became his sanctuary, Israel his
dominion. The sea saw it, and fled; Jordan turned back. The mountains skipped like
rams, the hills like lambs. What ails you, O you sea, that you flee? You Jordan, that you
turn back? You mountains that you skip like rams? You hills, like lambs? At the presence
of the Lord tremble, O earth, at the presence of the God of Jacob; who turned the rock
into a pool of water, the flint into a fountain of waters.

בְּצֵאת יִשְׂרָאֵל מִמִּצְרָיִם, בֵּית יַעֲקֹב מֵעַם לֹעֵז. הָיְתָה יְהוּדָה לְקָדְשׁוֹ, יִשְׂרָאֵל מַמְשְׁלוֹתָיו. הַיָּם רָאָה וַיָּנֹס, הַיַּרְדֵּן – יִסֹּב
לְאָחוֹר. הֶהָרִים רָקְדוּ כְאֵילִים, גְּבָעוֹת – כִּבְנֵי צֹאן. מַה לְּךָ, הַיָּם, כִּי תָנוּס? הַיַּרְדֵּן – תִּסֹּב לְאָחוֹר? הֶהָרִים, תִּרְקְדוּ
כְאֵילִים? גְּבָעוֹת – כִּבְנֵי צֹאן? מִלִּפְנֵי אָדוֹן חוּלִי, אָרֶץ, מִלִּפְנֵי אֱלוֹהַּ יַעֲקֹב. הַהֹפְכִי הַצּוּר אֲגַם מָיִם, חַלָּמִישׁ – לְמַעְיְנוֹ מָיִם.
(תְּהִלִּים קיד)

There are No Obstacles to Aliyah to the Land of Israel

When Rabbi Zeirach reached the border of the Land of Israel, he could find no ferry to carry him across the Jordan River.

A gentile said to him: You Jews are a rash people. You always place your mouth before your ears, as you said when the Torah was being given, We will do, before We will hear.

And you still cling to your rashness. Why couldn't you wait a little while longer and cross over by ferry?

Rabbi Zeirach said to him: Who is to say that I will be worthy of entering a land which both Moses and Aaron did not merit entering? Perhaps something will befall me before I enter the land.

Therefore, do I hurry, for the love of the land.

(According to the Exegesis of Rabbi Adin Steinsaltz to the Talmud: Ketuboth CXII, A)

The matzot are covered, the glass of wine is lifted up and the following is recited:

Blessed are You, O Lord, King of the Universe, who redeemed us, and redeemed our Fathers from Egypt, and enabled us to attain this night, on which to eat matzah and bitter herbs. Likewise, O Lord our God and God of our Fathers, enable us to reach other anniversaries and feasts (may they come to us in peace!), joyous in the building of Your city and exultant in Your service. There shall we partake of the festival sacrifices and of the paschal offerings,

If the night of the Seder falls on a Saturday evening, the following is recited: From the Paschal sacrifices and the festival offerings....

the blood of which shall be acceptably sprinkled upon the wall of Your altar; and there we will chant unto You a New Song, for our redemption and for our salvation. Blessed are You, O Lord, who redeemed Israel!

מְכַסִּים אֶת הַמַּצּוֹת, מַגְבִּיהִים אֶת כּוֹס הַיַּיִן וְאוֹמְרִים:

בָּרוּךְ

אַתָּה יְיָ, אֱלֹהֵינוּ מֶלֶךְ הָעוֹלָם, אֲשֶׁר גְּאָלָנוּ וְגָאַל אֶת אֲבוֹתֵינוּ מִמִּצְרַיִם וְהִגִּיעָנוּ לַלַּיְלָה הַזֶּה לֶאֱכָל־בּוֹ מַצָּה וּמָרוֹר. כֵּן יְיָ אֱלֹהֵינוּ וֵאלֹהֵי אֲבוֹתֵינוּ, יַגִּיעֵנוּ לְמוֹעֲדִים וְלִרְגָלִים אֲחֵרִים, הַבָּאִים לִקְרָאתֵנוּ לְשָׁלוֹם, שְׂמֵחִים בְּבִנְיַן עִירֶךָ, וְשָׂשִׂים בַּעֲבוֹדָתֶךָ, וְנֹאכַל שָׁם מִן הַזְּבָחִים וּמִן הַפְּסָחִים,

(אִם לֵיל הַסֵּדֶר חָל בְּמוֹצָאֵי שַׁבָּת, אוֹמְרִים: מִן הַפְּסָחִים וּמִן הַזְּבָחִים)

אֲשֶׁר יַגִּיעַ דָּמָם עַל קִיר מִזְבַּחֲךָ לְרָצוֹן, וְנוֹדֶה לְךָ שִׁיר חָדָשׁ עַל גְּאֻלָּתֵנוּ וְעַל פְּדוּת נַפְשֵׁנוּ. בָּרוּךְ אַתָּה יְיָ, גָּאַל יִשְׂרָאֵל.

The People of Israel will Last Forever

In the Torah it is written: And I will make your seed like the dust of the land (Genesis, XIII, 15). Just as the dust of the land exists from one end of the world to the other, so will your sons will be spread out from one end to the other.

And just as the dust of the land receives no blessing, other than by means of water, so the People of Israel are not blessed, other than through the merit of the Torah, which is compared to water.

And just as dust outlives all metal utensils and exists forever, so is it with the People of Israel. All the nations of the world pass on, while they remain everlasting.

(Bereshith [Genesis] Raba XL, 12)

Blessed are You, O Lord our God, King of the Universe, Creator of the fruit of the vine.

The wine is drunk while leaning to the left.

The hands are washed in the same way they were at the beginning of the Seder; this time, however, the following blessing is recited:

Blessed are You, our God, King of the Universe, who sanctified us by His commandments and commanded us concerning the washing of the hands.

The matzot are lifted up and two blessings are recited, Hamotzi and On the Eating of Matzah.

Blessed are You, O Lord our God, King of the Universe, who brings forth bread out of the earth.

יֵשׁ נוֹהֲגִים לוֹמַר בְּלַחַשׁ: הִנְנִי מוּכָן וּמְזֻמָּן לְקַיֵּם מִצְוַת כּוֹס שֵׁנִי מֵאַרְבַּע כּוֹסוֹת לְשֵׁם יְחוּד קֻדְשָׁא בְּרִיךְ הוּא וּשְׁכִינְתֵּהּ, עַל יְדֵי הַהוּא טָמִיר וְנֶעְלָם בְּשֵׁם כָּל יִשְׂרָאֵל.

בָּרוּךְ אַתָּה יְיָ, אֱלֹהֵינוּ מֶלֶךְ הָעוֹלָם, בּוֹרֵא פְּרִי הַגָּפֶן.

בָּרוּךְ אַתָּה יְיָ, אֱלֹהֵינוּ מֶלֶךְ הָעוֹלָם, **בּוֹרֵא פְּרִי הַגָּפֶן.**

רָחְצָה

שׁוֹתִים אֶת כּוֹס הַיַּיִן בַּהֲסִבַּת שְׂמֹאל.

רְחְצָה

נוֹטְלִים אֶת הַיָּדַיִם כְּפִי שֶׁנָּטְלוּ בִּתְחִלַּת הַסֵּדֶר, אֶלָּא שֶׁעַתָּה מְבָרְכִים:

בָּרוּךְ אַתָּה יְיָ, אֱלֹהֵינוּ מֶלֶךְ הָעוֹלָם, אֲשֶׁר קִדְּשָׁנוּ בְּמִצְוֹתָיו וְצִוָּנוּ עַל נְטִילַת יָדָיִם.

מוֹצִיא

מְרִימִים אֶת שְׁלוֹשׁ הַמַּצּוֹת וּמְבָרְכִים שְׁתֵּי בְּרָכוֹת: "הַמּוֹצִיא" וְ"עַל אֲכִילַת מַצָּה".

יֵשׁ נוֹהֲגִים גַּם לְהַגִּיד: הִנְנִי מוּכָן וּמְזֻמָּן לְקַיֵּם מִצְוַת אֲכִילַת מַצָּה לְשֵׁם יְחוּד קֻדְשָׁא בְּרִיךְ הוּא וּשְׁכִינְתֵּהּ, עַל יְדֵי הַהוּא טָמִיר וְנֶעְלָם בְּשֵׁם כָּל יִשְׂרָאֵל.

בָּרוּךְ אַתָּה יְיָ, אֱלֹהֵינוּ מֶלֶךְ הָעוֹלָם, הַמּוֹצִיא לֶחֶם מִן הָאָרֶץ.

The Land of Israel – A Bounteous Land

There is not even one vineyard in the Land of Israel which does not require a donkey colt at harvest time [in order to load the weight of the grapes cn it].
There is not even one barren tree in the Land of Israel that does not produce a yield to weigh down two she asses.

(Ketuboth, CXI, B)

The bottom matzah is put down, the other two matzot are held in hand, and the following blessing is recited, while leaning to the left:

Blessed are You, O Lord our God, King of the Universe, who sanctified us by His commandments and commanded us concerning the eating of matzah.

All dip the bitter herb in the haroset and say:

Blessed are You, O Lord our God, King of the Universe, who sanctified us by His commandments and commanded us concerning the eating of the bitter herb.

The bitter herb is eaten sitting up straight, without leaning.

An olive-sized portion of bitter herbs is picked up, and it is dipped in the haroseth. A blessing is recited and the mixture is eating, without leaning [to the left].

In remembrance of the Temple, according to the custom of Hillel. Hillel was accustomed to do thus when the Temple was still standing: he would place together some of the paschal sacrifice, matzah, and the bitter herb, and eat them as one, to fulfill that which is said: "Upon matzah and bitter herbs they shall eat it" *(Num. 9:11)*.

מַצָּה מַנִּיחִים אֶת הַמַּצָּה הַתַּחְתּוֹנָה, אוֹחֲזִים בִּשְׁתֵּי הָעֶלְיוֹנוֹת, וּמְבָרְכִים בַּהֲסִבָּה:

בָּרוּךְ אַתָּה יְיָ, אֱלֹהֵינוּ מֶלֶךְ הָעוֹלָם, אֲשֶׁר קִדְּשָׁנוּ בְּמִצְוֹתָיו וְצִוָּנוּ עַל אֲכִילַת מַצָּה.

אַחֲרֵי הַבְּרָכָה לוֹקְחִים חֲתִיכָה מֵהַמַּצָּה הָעֶלְיוֹנָה וַחֲתִיכָה מִן הַמַּצָּה הַתַּחְתּוֹנָה וְאוֹכְלִים אוֹתָן יַחַד.

מָרוֹר נוֹטְלִים כַּזַּיִת מָרוֹר, טוֹבְלִים בַּחֲרֹסֶת, מְבָרְכִים וְאוֹכְלִים בְּלִי הֲסִבָּה.

יֵשׁ נוֹהֲגִים גַּם לְהַגִּיד: הִנְנִי מוּכָן וּמְזֻמָּן לְקַיֵּם מִצְוַת אֲכִילַת מָרוֹר לְשֵׁם יִחוּד קֻדְשָׁא בְּרִיךְ הוּא וּשְׁכִינְתֵּהּ, עַל יְדֵי הַהוּא טָמִיר וְנֶעְלָם בְּשֵׁם כָּל יִשְׂרָאֵל.

בָּרוּךְ אַתָּה יְיָ, אֱלֹהֵינוּ מֶלֶךְ הָעוֹלָם, אֲשֶׁר קִדְּשָׁנוּ בְּמִצְוֹתָיו וְצִוָּנוּ עַל אֲכִילַת מָרוֹר.

כּוֹרֵךְ לוֹקְחִים כַּזַּיִת מִן הַמַּצָּה הַתַּחְתּוֹנָה, כּוֹרְכִים בְּתוֹכָהּ מָרוֹר, וְאוֹכְלִים בַּהֲסִבָּה וְאוֹמְרִים:

זֵכֶר לְמִקְדָּשׁ כְּהִלֵּל, כֵּן עָשָׂה הִלֵּל בִּזְמַן שֶׁבֵּית־הַמִּקְדָּשׁ הָיָה קַיָּם: הָיָה כּוֹרֵךְ מַצָּה וּמָרוֹר וְאוֹכֵל בְּיַחַד, לְקַיֵּם מַה שֶׁנֶּאֱמַר:
"עַל מַצּוֹת וּמְרֹרִים יֹאכְלֻהוּ". (בְּמִדְבַּר ט, יא)

Just as My Forefathers Planted for Me....

It is written of Hadrian, the Roman emperor who went to war at the head of his troops to do battle with a certain nation which had rebelled. He came across an old man by the side of the road, who was planting fig saplings.
The emperor said: You are old, yet you stand here and make an effort and tire yourself out for others.
The old man said: Your Highness, As you can see, I am planting. If I so merit, I shall eat of the fruits of my planting; if not, my sons will eat.

The emperor spent three years at war and then returned.
After three years had gone by he found the same old man at the same place.
What did the old man do? He took a basket and filled it with lovely figs which were the firstlings of his trees and approached Hadrian with this offering.
He said to him: Your Highness, receive this from your servant. I am that same old man whom you found when you passed by, and you said to me, you are old; why do you stand here and tire yourself out for others? As you can see, God has found me worthy to eat of the fruits of my planting, and those in the basket are your portion.
Immediately, Hadrian turned to his servants: Take the basket from him and fill it with gold coins, and do so....

So, will no man neglect his planting. Just as he found trees, so will he plant additional saplings, even though he be old.

(Midrash Tankhuma for Kedoshim, VIII)

שֻׁלְחָן עוֹרֵךְ

All eat the festive meal.

סוֹעֲדִים סְעוּדַת חַג. מֻתָּר לִשְׁתּוֹת יַיִן נוֹסָף עַל אַרְבַּע הַכּוֹסוֹת. וְיֵשׁ נוֹהֲגִים לְהַתְחִיל אֶת הָאֲרוּחָה בַּאֲכִילַת בֵּיצִים מְבֻשָּׁלוֹת.

צָפוּן

After the festive meal all eat a portion of the Afikoman.

אַחַר הַסְּעוּדָה מְחַפְּשִׂים אֶת הָאֲפִיקוֹמָן שֶׁהֶסְתַּר בִּתְחִלַּת הַסֵּדֶר. כָּל הַמִּשְׁתַּתְּפִים טוֹעֲמִים מִן הָאֲפִיקוֹמָן. יֵשׁ נוֹהֲגִים לוֹמַר: "הִנְנִי מוּכָן" וְאוֹכְלִים. הִנְנִי מוּכָן וּמְזֻמָּן לְקַיֵּם מִצְוַת אֲפִיקוֹמָן לְשֵׁם יִחוּד קֻדְשָׁא בְּרִיךְ הוּא וּשְׁכִינְתֵּהּ, עַל יְדֵי הַהוּא טָמִיר וְנֶעְלָם בְּשֵׁם כָּל יִשְׂרָאֵל.

מַה

The third glass of wine is poured.

מוֹזְגִים כּוֹס שְׁלִישִׁית מֵאַרְבַּע כּוֹסוֹת וּמְבָרְכִים בִּרְכַּת הַמָּזוֹן. נוֹהֲגִים לוֹמַר מִזְמוֹר תְּהִלִּים לִפְנֵי הַבְּרָכָה.

On the Rivers of Babylon

By the rivers of Babylon,
There we sat crying as we remembered Zion.
On the willows there we hung our harps,
For there our captors asked of us words of song, and our tormentors joy, saying,
Sing us of your songs of Zion.
How should we sing the song of the Lord on foreign soil?
If I forget you, Jerusalem, may my right hand wither;
My tongue cleave to the root of my mouth, if I do not remember you,
If I do not place Jerusalem above my highest joy.

(Psalms CXXXVII, 1-6)

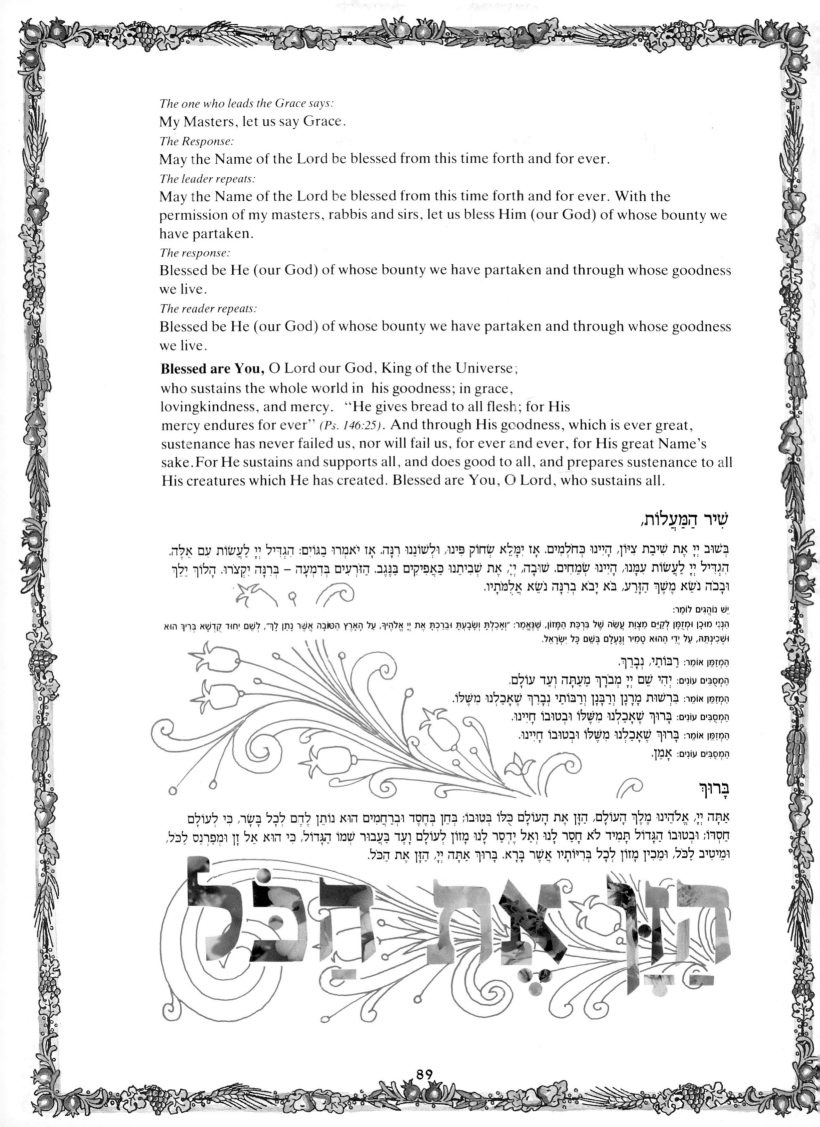

The one who leads the Grace says:

My Masters, let us say Grace.

The Response:

May the Name of the Lord be blessed from this time forth and for ever.

The leader repeats:

May the Name of the Lord be blessed from this time forth and for ever. With the permission of my masters, rabbis and sirs, let us bless Him (our God) of whose bounty we have partaken.

The response:

Blessed be He (our God) of whose bounty we have partaken and through whose goodness we live.

The reader repeats:

Blessed be He (our God) of whose bounty we have partaken and through whose goodness we live.

Blessed are You, O Lord our God, King of the Universe, who sustains the whole world in his goodness; in grace, lovingkindness, and mercy. "He gives bread to all flesh; for His mercy endures for ever" *(Ps. 146:25).* And through His goodness, which is ever great, sustenance has never failed us, nor will fail us, for ever and ever, for His great Name's sake. For He sustains and supports all, and does good to all, and prepares sustenance to all His creatures which He has created. Blessed are You, O Lord, who sustains all.

שִׁיר הַמַּעֲלוֹת,

בְּשׁוּב יְיָ אֶת שִׁיבַת צִיּוֹן, הָיִינוּ כְּחֹלְמִים. אָז יִמָּלֵא שְׂחוֹק פִּינוּ, וּלְשׁוֹנֵנוּ רִנָּה. אָז יֹאמְרוּ בַגּוֹיִם: הִגְדִּיל יְיָ לַעֲשׂוֹת עִם אֵלֶּה. הִגְדִּיל יְיָ לַעֲשׂוֹת עִמָּנוּ, הָיִינוּ שְׂמֵחִים. שׁוּבָה, יְיָ, אֶת שְׁבִיתֵנוּ כַּאֲפִיקִים בַּנֶּגֶב. הַזֹּרְעִים בְּדִמְעָה – בְּרִנָּה יִקְצֹרוּ. הָלוֹךְ יֵלֵךְ וּבָכֹה נֹשֵׂא מֶשֶׁךְ הַזָּרַע, בֹּא יָבֹא בְרִנָּה נֹשֵׂא אֲלֻמֹּתָיו.

יֵשׁ נוֹהֲגִים לוֹמַר:

הִנְנִי מוּכָן וּמְזֻמָּן לְקַיֵּם מִצְוַת עֲשֵׂה שֶׁל בִּרְכַּת הַמָּזוֹן, שֶׁנֶּאֱמַר: "וְאָכַלְתָּ וְשָׂבָעְתָּ וּבֵרַכְתָּ אֶת יְיָ אֱלֹהֶיךָ, עַל הָאָרֶץ הַטֹּבָה אֲשֶׁר נָתַן לָךְ", לְשֵׁם יִחוּד קֻדְשָׁא בְּרִיךְ הוּא וּשְׁכִינְתֵּהּ, עַל יְדֵי הַהוּא טָמִיר וְנֶעְלָם בְּשֵׁם כָּל יִשְׂרָאֵל.

הַמְזַמֵּן אוֹמֵר: רַבּוֹתַי, נְבָרֵךְ.

הַמְסֻבִּים עוֹנִים: יְהִי שֵׁם יְיָ מְבֹרָךְ מֵעַתָּה וְעַד עוֹלָם.

הַמְזַמֵּן אוֹמֵר: בִּרְשׁוּת מָרָנָן וְרַבָּנָן וְרַבּוֹתַי נְבָרֵךְ שֶׁאָכַלְנוּ מִשֶּׁלּוֹ.

הַמְסֻבִּים עוֹנִים: בָּרוּךְ שֶׁאָכַלְנוּ מִשֶּׁלּוֹ וּבְטוּבוֹ חָיִינוּ.

הַמְזַמֵּן אוֹמֵר: בָּרוּךְ שֶׁאָכַלְנוּ מִשֶּׁלּוֹ וּבְטוּבוֹ חָיִינוּ.

הַמְסֻבִּים עוֹנִים: אָמֵן.

בָּרוּךְ

אַתָּה יְיָ, אֱלֹהֵינוּ מֶלֶךְ הָעוֹלָם, הַזָּן אֶת הָעוֹלָם כֻּלּוֹ בְּטוּבוֹ: בְּחֵן בְּחֶסֶד וּבְרַחֲמִים הוּא נוֹתֵן לֶחֶם לְכָל בָּשָׂר, כִּי לְעוֹלָם חַסְדּוֹ; וּבְטוּבוֹ הַגָּדוֹל תָּמִיד לֹא חָסַר לָנוּ וְאַל יֶחְסַר לָנוּ מָזוֹן לְעוֹלָם וָעֶד בַּעֲבוּר שְׁמוֹ הַגָּדוֹל, כִּי הוּא אֵל זָן וּמְפַרְנֵס לַכֹּל, וּמֵיטִיב לַכֹּל, וּמֵכִין מָזוֹן לְכָל בְּרִיּוֹתָיו אֲשֶׁר בָּרָא. בָּרוּךְ אַתָּה יְיָ, הַזָּן אֶת הַכֹּל.

A Song of Ascent

A song of ascent for David
I was happy when they said to me, Let us go to the House of the Lord.
Our feet were standing within your gates, Jerusalem,
Jerusalem, built up as a city bound together,
To which the tribes ascend, The tribes of the Lord,
Evidence of their being Israel, To give thanks to the name of the Lord.
For there thrones of judgment were set, the chairs of the House of David.
Pray for the peace of Jerusalem, may those who love you, find peace.
For the sake of my brothers and friends, I will say, peace be with you....

(Psalms, CXXII, 1-8)

Let us render thanks unto You, O Lord our God, because You gave us an inheritance to our fathers; a land which is pleasant, goodly and ample; and because You brought us forth, O Lord our God, from the land of Egypt, and redeemed us from the house of bondage; and for Your covenant which You sealed in our flesh, and for Your Torah which You taught us, and for Your statute which You made known unto us, and for the life, grace and lovingkindness with which You have favored us, and for this sustenance with which You sustain and support us continually – on every day, and at every time, and in every hour.

For all this, O Lord our God, we render thanks to You and bless You. Blessed be Your Name in the mouth of all that lives, continually and for evermore; as it is written: "And you shall eat, and be satisfied, and shall bless your Lord your God for the good land which He has given you" *(Deut. 8:10)*. Blessed are You, O Lord, for the Land and for the sustenance.

נוֹדֶה

לְךָ, יְיָ אֱלֹהֵינוּ, עַל שֶׁהִנְחַלְתָּ לַאֲבוֹתֵינוּ אֶרֶץ חֶמְדָּה טוֹבָה וּרְחָבָה, וְעַל שֶׁהוֹצֵאתָנוּ, יְיָ אֱלֹהֵינוּ, מֵאֶרֶץ מִצְרַיִם וּפְדִיתָנוּ מִבֵּית־עֲבָדִים, וְעַל בְּרִיתְךָ שֶׁחָתַמְתָּ בִּבְשָׂרֵנוּ, וְעַל תּוֹרָתְךָ שֶׁלִּמַּדְתָּנוּ וְעַל חֻקֶּיךָ שֶׁהוֹדַעְתָּנוּ, וְעַל חַיִּים, חֵן וָחֶסֶד שֶׁחוֹנַנְתָּנוּ, וְעַל אֲכִילַת מָזוֹן, שָׁאַתָּה זָן וּמְפַרְנֵס אוֹתָנוּ תָּמִיד, בְּכָל יוֹם וּבְכָל עֵת וּבְכָל שָׁעָה.

וְעַל הַכֹּל,

יְיָ אֱלֹהֵינוּ, אֲנַחְנוּ מוֹדִים לָךְ וּמְבָרְכִים אוֹתָךְ, יִתְבָּרַךְ שִׁמְךָ בְּפִי כָּל חַי תָּמִיד לְעוֹלָם וָעֶד, כַּכָּתוּב: "וְאָכַלְתָּ וְשָׂבָעְתָּ וּבֵרַכְתָּ אֶת יְיָ אֱלֹהֶיךָ עַל הָאָרֶץ הַטֹּבָה, אֲשֶׁר נָתַן לָךְ". בָּרוּךְ אַתָּה יְיָ, עַל הָאָרֶץ וְעַל הַמָּזוֹן.

עַל הָאָרֶץ וְעַל הַמָּזוֹן

Jerusalem – The Center of a Jew's World

When people outside the Land of Israel pray, they turn their faces to the Land of Israel – to the East – as it is written: And they pray to You in the direction of their land. (I Kings, VIII, 48)
Those who are in the Land of Israel turn their faces towards Jerusalem when they pray, as it is written: And they pray to You in the direction of this city. (I Chronicles VI)

Those who are in the North turn their faces southward, and those in the South turn their faces northward. Those who are in the East turn their faces westward, and those who are in the West turn their faces northward.
Thus, all of the People of Israel pray in the direction of the same place.

(Shir Hashirim [Song of Songs] Raba IV, 11)

Have mercy, O Lord our God, upon Israel Your people, and upon Jerusalem Your city, and upon Zion the abiding-place of Your glory, and upon the kingdom of the house of David, Your anointed, and upon the great and holy House which is called by Your Name. O our God, our Father! Lead us, sustain us, support us, maintain us, and deliver us! Deliver us, O Lord our God, speedily from all our troubles. And we beseech You, O Lord our God, do not make us dependent upon the gifts of flesh and blood, nor upon their loans, but only upon Your full, open, holy and ample hand; so that we may not be ashamed nor abashed for ever and ever.

On the Sabbath, the following is added:

Be pleased, O Lord our God, to sustain us by Your precepts, and especially by the precept concerning the seventh day, the great and holy Sabbath. For this day is great and holy before You, that we may rest and repose on it lovingly, according to Your gracious precept. By Your grace, O Lord our God, grant us repose, that there may be no trouble nor sorrow nor lamentation upon our day of rest; and cause us to see the consolation of Zion, Your city, and the building of Jerusalem Your holy city; for You are He who is Lord of redemption and Lord of consolation.

רַחֶם־נָא,

יְיָ אֱלֹהֵינוּ, עַל יִשְׂרָאֵל עַמֶּךָ, וְעַל יְרוּשָׁלַיִם עִירֶךָ, וְעַל צִיּוֹן מִשְׁכַּן כְּבוֹדֶךָ, וְעַל מַלְכוּת בֵּית דָּוִד מְשִׁיחֶךָ, וְעַל הַבַּיִת הַגָּדוֹל וְהַקָּדוֹשׁ שֶׁנִּקְרָא שִׁמְךָ עָלָיו. אֱלֹהֵינוּ אָבִינוּ, רְעֵנוּ, זוּנֵנוּ, פַּרְנְסֵנוּ וְכַלְכְּלֵנוּ וְהַרְוִיחֵנוּ וְהַרְוַח לָנוּ, יְיָ אֱלֹהֵינוּ, מְהֵרָה מִכָּל צָרוֹתֵינוּ. וְנָא אַל תַּצְרִיכֵנוּ, יְיָ אֱלֹהֵינוּ, לֹא לִידֵי מַתְּנַת בָּשָׂר־וָדָם וְלֹא לִידֵי הַלְוָאָתָם, כִּי אִם לְיָדְךָ הַמְּלֵאָה, הַפְּתוּחָה, הַקְּדוֹשָׁה וְהָרְחָבָה, שֶׁלֹּא נֵבוֹשׁ וְלֹא נִכָּלֵם לְעוֹלָם וָעֶד.

בְּשַׁבָּת מוֹסִיפִים:

רְצֵה

וְהַחֲלִיצֵנוּ, יְיָ אֱלֹהֵינוּ, בְּמִצְוֹתֶיךָ וּבְמִצְוַת יוֹם הַשְּׁבִיעִי, הַשַּׁבָּת הַגָּדוֹל וְהַקָּדוֹשׁ הַזֶּה, כִּי יוֹם זֶה גָּדוֹל וְקָדוֹשׁ הוּא לְפָנֶיךָ לִשְׁבָּת־בּוֹ, וְלָנוּחַ בּוֹ בְּאַהֲבָה כְּמִצְוַת רְצוֹנֶךָ; וּבִרְצוֹנְךָ הָנִיחַ לָנוּ, יְיָ אֱלֹהֵינוּ, שֶׁלֹּא תְהֵא צָרָה וְיָגוֹן וַאֲנָחָה בְּיוֹם מְנוּחָתֵנוּ, וְהַרְאֵנוּ, יְיָ אֱלֹהֵינוּ, בְּנֶחָמַת צִיּוֹן עִירֶךָ וּבְבִנְיַן יְרוּשָׁלַיִם עִיר קָדְשֶׁךָ, כִּי אַתָּה הוּא בַּעַל הַיְשׁוּעוֹת וּבַעַל הַנֶּחָמוֹת.

In Jerusalem — the Foundation of the World

The entire world is encompassed in Zion.
Why is Zion called the foundation stone upon the world is based?
Just as the navel is located in the center of the human being, so the Land of Israel is located in the center of the universe, as it is written:
Dwellers at the center of the earth. (Ezekiel XXXVIII, 12)

The Land of Israel is situated at the center of the universe,
And Jerusalem at the center of the Land of Israel,
And the Temple at the center of Jerusalem,
And the Holy of Holies at the center of the Temple,
And the Ark of the Law at the center of the Holy of Holies, And the foundation stone before the Ark of the Law,
Upon which the world is based.
And Solomon, who was wise, stood on the roots which emanate from Jerusalem to the entire world and planted in that city all sorts of fruit-bearing trees.

(Midrash Tankhuma for Kedoshim, X)

Our God, and God of our Fathers! May there ascend, and come, and arrive, and be seen, and accepted, and heard, and visited, and remembered – our remembrance, and our visitation, and the remembrance of our Fathers, and the remembrance of the anointed Messiah, son of David Your servant, and the remembrance of Jerusalem Your Holy city, **and the remembrance of the whole of Your people the house of Israel;** for deliverance, and for good, and for grace, and for lovingkindness, and for mercy, and for life, and for peace, before You, upon this day, the Feast of Matzot. Remember us on it, O Lord, for good, and visit us on it for a blessing, and save us on it for life; through tidings of redemption and mercy pity us and show us grace, and be merciful unto us and redeem us, for to You are our eyes turned, for You are a gracious and merciful God and King.

אֱלֹהֵינוּ

וֵאלֹהֵי אֲבוֹתֵינוּ, יַעֲלֶה וְיָבֹא וְיַגִּיעַ וְיֵרָאֶה וְיֵרָצֶה וְיִשָּׁמַע וְיִפָּקֵד וְיִזָּכֵר זִכְרוֹנֵנוּ וּפִקְדוֹנֵנוּ, וְזִכְרוֹן אֲבוֹתֵינוּ, וְזִכְרוֹן מָשִׁיחַ בֶּן דָּוִד עַבְדֶּךָ, וְזִכְרוֹן יְרוּשָׁלַיִם עִיר קָדְשֶׁךָ, וְזִכְרוֹן כָּל עַמְּךָ בֵּית יִשְׂרָאֵל לְפָנֶיךָ לִפְלֵיטָה, לְטוֹבָה, לְחֵן וּלְחֶסֶד וּלְרַחֲמִים, לְחַיִּים וּלְשָׁלוֹם, בְּיוֹם חַג הַמַּצּוֹת הַזֶּה. זָכְרֵנוּ, יְיָ אֱלֹהֵינוּ, בּוֹ לְטוֹבָה, וּפָקְדֵנוּ בוֹ לִבְרָכָה, וְהוֹשִׁיעֵנוּ בוֹ לְחַיִּים. וּבִדְבַר יְשׁוּעָה וְרַחֲמִים חוּס וְחָנֵּנוּ וְרַחֵם עָלֵינוּ וְהוֹשִׁיעֵנוּ, כִּי אֵלֶיךָ עֵינֵינוּ, כִּי אֵל מֶלֶךְ חַנּוּן וְרַחוּם אָתָּה.

The Connection and Devotion to Jerusalem

I shall choose to spill my soul in that place where
The Spirit of God has been spilt on Its chosen ones....

Would that I roam in those places where
God was revealed to your prophets and emissaries.
Who will lend me wings, that I'll wander far,
That I'll speak to my broken heart among your broken pieces.
I'll prostrate myself on your land;
I'll desire your stones greatly and favor your dust.

(Yehuda Halevi)

וּבְנֵה יְרוּשָׁלַיִם

עִיר הַקֹּדֶשׁ

AND BUILD JERUSALEM
THE HOLY CITY

speedily in our days; blessed are You, O Lord, Rebuilder, in His mercy,
of Jerusalem, Amen!

וּבְנֵה יְרוּשָׁלַיִם עִיר הַקֹּדֶשׁ בִּמְהֵרָה בְיָמֵינוּ. בָּרוּךְ אַתָּה יְיָ, בּוֹנֵה בְרַחֲמָיו יְרוּשָׁלַיִם אָמֵן.

A New Land

For behold, I am creating a new heaven and a new earth,
And the earlier ones will not be remembered or brought to mind.
However, you will rejoice and be glad forever in what I create,
For behold, I am creating a glad Jerusalem and her people joyous.
And I will rejoice in Jerusalem and be glad in my people,
and no longer will the voice of crying
and the voice of distress be heard.
No longer will there be children there who die in infancy,
or elderly people who do not live out their allotted days,
for the child shall die at the age of one hundred, and the sinner,
one hundred years old, will be cursed.
And they shall build houses and inhabit them,
and plant vineyards and eat of their fruits.
They will not build for others to inhabit;
they will not plant for others to eat.
For like the days of a tree, the days of my people will be, and my
chosen ones will enjoy the work of their hands for many years.

(Isaiah LXV, 17-22)

Blessed are You, O Lord our God, King of the Universe; O God, our Father, our King, our Mighty One, our Creator, our Redeemer, our Maker, our Holy One, the Holy One of Jacob; our Shepherd, the **Shepherd of Israel;** the good King, who does good to all,

who, upon every day did good, does good, and will do good unto us. He has bestowed and He does bestow benefits upon us always, for grace, lovingkindness, mercy and deliverance; protection, prosperity, blessing, salvation, comfort, support, sustenance, mercy, life, peace and all good; and may He never let us lack all good!

May the All-Merciful reign over us, for ever and ever! May the All-Merciful be blessed in heaven and on earth! May the All-Merciful be praised for all generations, and may He be glorified through us for all ages, and exalted through us for ever, and for all eternity! May the All-Merciful grant us honorable sustenance! May the All-Merciful break the yoke from off our neck, and may He lead us upright to our land! May the All-Merciful send an ample blessing to this house, and upon this table whereon we have eaten! May the All-Merciful send us Elijah the Prophet (may he be remembered for good!), who shall proclaim us good tidings, salvation and comfort.

May the All-Merciful bless all that sit here – them, their household, their offspring, and all that is theirs; us, and all that is ours. As our fathers Abraham, Isaac, and Jacob were blessed "in all" *(Gen. 24:1)* "of all" *(27:33)*, "in respect of all" *(33:11)*, so may He bless us all together with a perfect blessing; and let us say, **Amen!**

בָּרוּךְ

אַתָּה יְיָ, אֱלֹהֵינוּ מֶלֶךְ הָעוֹלָם, הָאֵל אָבִינוּ, מַלְכֵּנוּ, אַדִּירֵנוּ, בּוֹרְאֵנוּ, גּוֹאֲלֵנוּ, יוֹצְרֵנוּ, קְדוֹשֵׁנוּ, קְדוֹשׁ יַעֲקֹב, רוֹעֵנוּ, רוֹעֵה

יִשְׂרָאֵל; הַמֶּלֶךְ הַטּוֹב וְהַמֵּטִיב לַכֹּל, שֶׁבְּכָל יוֹם וָיוֹם הוּא הֵיטִיב, הוּא מֵטִיב, הוּא יֵיטִיב לָנוּ; הוּא גְמָלָנוּ, הוּא גוֹמְלֵנוּ, הוּא

יִגְמְלֵנוּ לָעַד, לְחֵן וּלְחֶסֶד וּלְרַחֲמִים וּלְרֶוַח, הַצָּלָה וְהַצְלָחָה, בְּרָכָה וִישׁוּעָה, נֶחָמָה, פַּרְנָסָה וְכַלְכָּלָה, וְרַחֲמִים וְחַיִּים וְשָׁלוֹם

וְכָל טוֹב, וּמִכָּל טוּב לְעוֹלָם אַל יְחַסְּרֵנוּ.

הָרַחֲמָן, הוּא יִמְלֹךְ עָלֵינוּ לְעוֹלָם וָעֶד.

הָרַחֲמָן, הוּא יִתְבָּרַךְ בַּשָּׁמַיִם וּבָאָרֶץ.

הָרַחֲמָן, הוּא יִשְׁתַּבַּח לְדוֹר דּוֹרִים וְיִתְפָּאַר בָּנוּ לָעַד וּלְנֵצַח נְצָחִים וְיִתְהַדַּר בָּנוּ לָעַד וּלְעוֹלְמֵי עוֹלָמִים.

הָרַחֲמָן, הוּא יְפַרְנְסֵנוּ בְּכָבוֹד.

הָרַחֲמָן, הוּא יִשְׁבֹּר עֻלֵּנוּ מֵעַל צַוָּארֵנוּ וְהוּא יוֹלִיכֵנוּ קוֹמְמִיּוּת לְאַרְצֵנוּ.

הָרַחֲמָן, הוּא יִשְׁלַח לָנוּ בְּרָכָה מְרֻבָּה בַּבַּיִת הַזֶּה וְעַל שֻׁלְחָן זֶה שֶׁאָכַלְנוּ עָלָיו.

הָרַחֲמָן, הוּא יִשְׁלַח לָנוּ אֶת אֵלִיָּהוּ הַנָּבִיא, זָכוּר לַטּוֹב, וִיבַשֶּׂר-לָנוּ בְּשׂוֹרוֹת טוֹבוֹת, יְשׁוּעוֹת וְנֶחָמוֹת.

הָרַחֲמָן, הוּא יְבָרֵךְ אֶת (אם יֵשׁ לוֹ אָב וְאֵם:) אָבִי מוֹרִי (בַּעַל הַבַּיִת הַזֶּה) וְאֶת (אִמִּי מוֹרָתִי) בַּעֲלַת הַבַּיִת הַזֶּה אוֹתָם וְאֶת בֵּיתָם

וְאֶת זַרְעָם וְאֶת כָּל אֲשֶׁר לָהֶם. (אם הַמְבָרֵךְ נָשׂוּי, יֹאמַר:) אוֹתִי וְאֶת אִשְׁתִּי וְאֶת זַרְעִי וְאֶת כָּל אֲשֶׁר לִי), אוֹתָנוּ וְאֶת כָּל אֲשֶׁר

לָנוּ, כְּמוֹ שֶׁנִּתְבָּרְכוּ אֲבוֹתֵינוּ אַבְרָהָם, יִצְחָק וְיַעֲקֹב "בַּכֹּל", "מִכֹּל", "כֹּל", כֵּן יְבָרֵךְ אוֹתָנוּ, כֻּלָּנוּ יַחַד, בִּבְרָכָה שְׁלֵמָה,

וְנֹאמַר: אָמֵן.

Redemption

Therefore, behold, says the Lord, the days are coming when no longer will it be said, As lives the Lord who brought the People of Israel out of the Land of Egypt. Rather, As lives the Lord who led and brought the descendants of the House of Israel from the land to the North and from all the lands into which I had driven them. And they will settle their own land.

(Jeremiah, XXIII, 7-8)

Upon high, may merit be found for us, which shall be for a store of peace; and may we receive a blessing from the Lord, and righteousness from the God of our salvation, so that we may find grace and good understanding in the sight of God and men!

On the Sabbath, the following is recited:

May the All-Merciful cause us to inherit that day which shall be altogether Sabbath and repose, in everlasting life!
May the All-Merciful cause us to inherit that day which shall be altogether a Holy Day!
May the All-Merciful make us worthy of the days of the Messiah and the life of the world to come!
"He is a tower of deliverance to His King, and shows lovingkindness to His anointed, to David and to his seed, for evermore!" *(II Sam, 22:51)*. He who makes peace in His high places, may He make **peace for us and for all Israel; and say you,** Amen!

בַּמָּרוֹם

יְלַמְּדוּ עֲלֵיהֶם וְעָלֵינוּ זְכוּת שֶׁתְּהֵא לְמִשְׁמֶרֶת שָׁלוֹם, "וְנִשָּׂא בְרָכָה מֵאֵת יְיָ וּצְדָקָה מֵאֱלֹהֵי יִשְׁעֵנוּ", "וְנִמְצָא חֵן וְשֵׂכֶל טוֹב בְּעֵינֵי אֱלֹהִים וְאָדָם".

בְּשַׁבָּת מוֹסִיפִים: הָרַחֲמָן, הוּא יַנְחִילֵנוּ יוֹם שֶׁכֻּלּוֹ שַׁבָּת וּמְנוּחָה לְחַיֵּי הָעוֹלָמִים.
הָרַחֲמָן, הוּא יַנְחִילֵנוּ יוֹם שֶׁכֻּלּוֹ טוֹב.

הָרַחֲמָן,

הוּא יְזַכֵּנוּ לִימוֹת הַמָּשִׁיחַ וּלְחַיֵּי הָעוֹלָם הַבָּא. "מִגְדּוֹל יְשׁוּעוֹת מַלְכּוֹ וְעֹשֶׂה חֶסֶד לִמְשִׁיחוֹ", לְדָוִד וּלְזַרְעוֹ עַד עוֹלָם". עֹשֶׂה שָׁלוֹם בִּמְרוֹמָיו הוּא יַעֲשֶׂה שָׁלוֹם עָלֵינוּ וְעַל כָּל יִשְׂרָאֵל, וְאִמְרוּ: אָמֵן.

Redemption

Lift up your eyes and look about and see,
They have all gathered together, they are coming to you.
Your sons will come from afar and your daughters brought
as though coming alongside their tutors.

Then you will see and be radiant, be fearful, but then your
heart will rejoice, For a multitude of people from the lands
of the seas will turn towards you, The wealth of nations
come to you.... Who are these, flying like a cloud and
like doves to the windows of their dovecotes?

(Isaiah LX, 4-5; 8)

"**Fear the Lord,** His saints, for there is no want to them that fear Him. The young lions lack, and suffer hunger, but they that seek the Lord shall not want any good thing" *(Ps. 34:9-10)*. "O give thanks unto the Lord, for He is good, for His mercy endures for ever" *(Ps. 118:1)*. "You open Your hand and satisfy every living thing with favor" *(Ps. 145:16)*. "Blessed is the man that trusts in the Lord, and whose trust the Lord is" *(Ps. 40:4)*. "I have been young and now am old; yet I have not seen the righteous forsaken nor his seed begging for bread" *(Ps. 37:25)*. "The Lord will give strength unto His people; the Lord will bless His people with peace" *(Ps. 29:11)*.

All take the third cup of wine, recite the blessing below, and then drink the wine while leaning to the left:
Blessed are You, O Lord our God, King of the Universe, Creator of the fruit of the vine.

The fourth glass is poured, as is the cup of Elijah the Prophet.

It is customary to ask one of the Seder participants to open the door for Elijah the Prophet. There are those whose custom it is to say, Baruch Habah – Welcome – when the door is opened.

"POUR OUT YOUR WRATH UPON THE HEATHEN that have not known You, and upon the kingdoms that have not called upon Your Name; for they have devoured Jacob and laid waste his dwelling place" *(Ps. 76:6)*. "Pour out upon them Your indignation and let Your fierce anger overtake them" *(Ps. 64:25)*. "Pursue them in wrath and destroy them from under the heavens of the Lord" *(Lam. 3:66)*.

The door is closed

יְראוּ אֶת יְיָ קְדֹשָׁיו, כִּי אֵין מַחְסוֹר לִירֵאָיו. כְּפִירִים רָשׁוּ וְרָעֵבוּ, וְדֹרְשֵׁי יְיָ לֹא יַחְסְרוּ כָל טוֹב. הוֹדוּ לַיְיָ כִּי טוֹב, כִּי לְעוֹלָם חַסְדּוֹ. פּוֹתֵחַ אֶת יָדֶךָ וּמַשְׂבִּיעַ לְכָל חַי רָצוֹן. בָּרוּךְ הַגֶּבֶר אֲשֶׁר יִבְטַח בַּיְיָ, וְהָיָה יְיָ מִבְטַחוֹ. נַעַר הָיִיתִי גַּם זָקַנְתִּי, וְלֹא רָאִיתִי צַדִּיק נֶעֱזָב וְזַרְעוֹ מְבַקֶּשׁ לָחֶם. יְיָ עֹז לְעַמּוֹ יִתֵּן, יְיָ יְבָרֵךְ אֶת עַמּוֹ בַשָּׁלוֹם.

יֵשׁ נוֹהֲגִים לְהַגִּיד:

הִנְנִי מוּכָן וּמְזֻמָּן לְקַיֵּם מִצְוַת כּוֹס שְׁלִישִׁי כּוֹס מֵאַרְבַּע כּוֹסוֹת לְשֵׁם יִחוּד קֻדְשָׁא בְּרִיךְ הוּא וּשְׁכִינְתֵּהּ, עַל יְדֵי הַהוּא טָמִיר וְנֶעֱלָם בְּשֵׁם כָּל יִשְׂרָאֵל. מְבָרְכִים בְּקוֹל:

בָּרוּךְ אַתָּה יְיָ, אֱלֹהֵינוּ מֶלֶךְ הָעוֹלָם, בּוֹרֵא פְּרִי הַגָּפֶן.

מוֹזְגִים כּוֹס רְבִיעִית וְאֶת כּוֹסוֹ שֶׁל אֵלִיָּהוּ הַנָּבִיא.

נוֹהֲגִים לְבַקֵּשׁ מֵאֶחָד הַמִּשְׁתַּתְּפִים בַּסֵּדֶר לִפְתֹּחַ אֶת הַדֶּלֶת לְאֵלִיָּהוּ הַנָּבִיא. יֵשׁ נוֹהֲגִים לוֹמַר בִּשְׁעַת פְּתִיחַת הַדֶּלֶת "בָּרוּךְ הַבָּא".

שְׁפֹךְ חֲמָתְךָ אֶל הַגּוֹיִם, אֲשֶׁר לֹא יְדָעוּךָ, וְעַל מַמְלָכוֹת, אֲשֶׁר בְּשִׁמְךָ לֹא קָרָאוּ. כִּי אָכַל אֶת יַעֲקֹב וְאֶת נָוֵהוּ הֵשַׁמּוּ.

שְׁפָךְ עֲלֵיהֶם זַעֲמֶךָ, וַחֲרוֹן אַפְּךָ יַשִּׂיגֵם. תִּרְדֹּף בְּאַף וְתַשְׁמִידֵם מִתַּחַת שְׁמֵי יְיָ. (תְּהִלִּים עט, ו-ז; תְּהִלִּים סט, כה)

סוֹגְרִים אֶת הַדֶּלֶת.

The Land of Israel and the Ingathering of the Diaspora

The big Rabbi Hiya and Rabbi Shimon ben Halafta were walking in the Arbel Valley, and they saw the morning star appear.

Rabbi Hiya said to Rabbi Shimon: I swear by my rabbi, thus will Israel be redeemed — little by little at first. The more it appears, the stronger it appears.

(Jerusalem Talmud, Brahot, LXXXI, Halacha A)

Psalm 115:

NOT UNTO US, O Lord, but unto Your Name give glory, for Your lovingkindness and for Your truth's sake. Why should the nations say, Where, then, is their God? But our God is in the heavens, He does whatsoever He pleases. Their idols are silver and gold, the work of men's hands. They have mouths, but they speak not; eyes have they, but they see not. They have ears, but they hear not; noses have they, but they smell not. As for their hands, they touch not, as for their feet, they walk not; they give no sound through their throat. They that make them shall be like unto them; and everyone that trusts in them.

O Israel, trust in the Lord; He is their help and their shield. O house of Aaron, trust in the Lord; He is their help and their shield. You that fear the Lord, trust in the Lord; He is their help and their shield.

The Lord has remembered us; He will bless, He will bless the house of Israel; He will bless the house of Aaron. He will bless those that fear the Lord, both small and great. May the Lord increase you, you and your children. Blessed are you of the Lord, who made heaven and earth. The heavens are the heavens of the Lord; but the earth He has given to the children of men. The dead do not praise the Lord, neither any that go down in silence; but we will bless the Lord from this time forth and for evermore.

HALLELUYAH!

הַלֵּל

לֹא לָנוּ, יְיָ, לֹא לָנוּ, כִּי לְשִׁמְךָ תֵּן כָּבוֹד, עַל חַסְדְּךָ, עַל אֲמִתֶּךָ. לָמָה יֹאמְרוּ הַגּוֹיִם: אַיֵּה נָא אֱלֹהֵיהֶם? וֵאלֹהֵינוּ בַשָּׁמַיִם, כֹּל אֲשֶׁר חָפֵץ עָשָׂה. עֲצַבֵּיהֶם כֶּסֶף וְזָהָב, מַעֲשֵׂה יְדֵי אָדָם. פֶּה לָהֶם וְלֹא יְדַבֵּרוּ, עֵינַיִם לָהֶם וְלֹא יִרְאוּ. אָזְנַיִם לָהֶם וְלֹא יִשְׁמָעוּ, אַף לָהֶם וְלֹא יְרִיחוּן. יְדֵיהֶם וְלֹא יְמִישׁוּן, רַגְלֵיהֶם וְלֹא יְהַלֵּכוּ, לֹא יֶהְגּוּ בִּגְרוֹנָם. כְּמוֹהֶם יִהְיוּ עֹשֵׂיהֶם, כֹּל אֲשֶׁר בֹּטֵחַ בָּהֶם.

יִשְׂרָאֵל, בְּטַח בַּיְיָ, עֶזְרָם וּמָגִנָּם הוּא.

בֵּית אַהֲרֹן, בִּטְחוּ בַיְיָ, עֶזְרָם וּמָגִנָּם הוּא.

יִרְאֵי יְיָ בִּטְחוּ בַיְיָ, עֶזְרָם וּמָגִנָּם הוּא.

יְיָ זְכָרָנוּ,

יְבָרֵךְ, יְבָרֵךְ אֶת בֵּית יִשְׂרָאֵל, יְבָרֵךְ אֶת בֵּית אַהֲרֹן. יְבָרֵךְ יִרְאֵי יְיָ, הַקְּטַנִּים עִם הַגְּדֹלִים. יֹסֵף יְיָ עֲלֵיכֶם, עֲלֵיכֶם וְעַל בְּנֵיכֶם. בְּרוּכִים אַתֶּם לַיְיָ, עֹשֵׂה שָׁמַיִם וָאָרֶץ. הַשָּׁמַיִם – שָׁמַיִם לַיְיָ, וְהָאָרֶץ נָתַן לִבְנֵי אָדָם. לֹא הַמֵּתִים יְהַלְלוּ יָהּ, וְלֹא כָּל יֹרְדֵי דוּמָה. וַאֲנַחְנוּ נְבָרֵךְ יָהּ מֵעַתָּה וְעַד עוֹלָם, הַלְלוּיָהּ. (תְּהִלִּים קטו)

The Torah & the People of Israel

Eliyahu said: Once, when I used to wander from place to place, I found a man who said to me: There are two things in the world which I love without reservation, and they are the Torah and the People of Israel. But I do not know which one comes first.

I said to him: My son, it is the habit of people to say, the Torah comes first;

But I say, the People of Israel come first, as it is written: The People of Israel are holy to the Lord, the first fruits of His harvest. (Jeremiah II, 3)

It may be compared to a king, whose wife and sons lived in his house. And he directed a writ to the place where his wife and sons were: Were it not for my wife and sons, who are a source of contentment for me in the house, I would have razed the place.

Thus, were it not for the People of Israel, the universe would not have been created, and it surely would have been destroyed.

(Tana Rabbi Eliyahu, XIV)

Psalm 116: **I LOVE THE LORD,** because He hears my voice and my supplications. Because He has inclined His ear unto me, I will call upon Him as long as I live. The cords of death had encompassed me, and the straits of the grave had come upon me; I found trouble and sorrow. Then I called upon the Name of the Lord. O Lord: I beseech You, deliver my soul.

Gracious is the Lord and righteous; our God is merciful. The Lord guards the simple; I was brought low, and He saved me. Return unto your rest, O my soul; for the Lord has dealt bountifully with you. For You have delivered my soul from death, my eyes from tears, my feet from falling. I shall walk before the Lord in the land of the living. I kept my faith in God even when I spoke, I was greatly afflicted; even when I said in my haste, All men are liars.

What can I render unto the Lord for all his benefits towards me? I will lift the cup of salvation and call upon the Name of the Lord. I will pay my vows unto the Lord, in the presence of all His people. Precious in the sight of the Lord is the death of His loving ones.

Ah, Lord, truly I am Your servant; I am Your servant, the son, of Your handmaiden; You have loosened my bonds. I will offer to You the sacrifice of thanksgiving, and will call upon the Name of the Lord. I will pay my vows unto the Lord, in the presence of all His people; in the courts of the Lord's house, in the midst of you, O Jerusalem,

HALLELUYAH!

Psalm 117: O PRAISE THE LORD, all you nations; laud Him, all you peoples; for His lovingkindness is mighty over us, and the truth of the Lord endures for ever. Halleluyah!

אָהַבְתִּי

כִּי יִשְׁמַע יְיָ אֶת קוֹלִי, תַּחֲנוּנָי. כִּי הִטָּה אָזְנוֹ לִי, וּבְיָמַי אֶקְרָא. אֲפָפוּנִי חֶבְלֵי מָוֶת, וּמְצָרֵי שְׁאוֹל מְצָאוּנִי, צָרָה וְיָגוֹן אֶמְצָא. וּבְשֵׁם יְיָ אֶקְרָא: אָנָּה, יְיָ מַלְּטָה נַפְשִׁי. חַנּוּן יְיָ וְצַדִּיק, וֵאלֹהֵינוּ מְרַחֵם. שֹׁמֵר פְּתָאיִם יְיָ, דַּלּוֹתִי וְלִי יְהוֹשִׁיעַ. שׁוּבִי נַפְשִׁי לִמְנוּחָיְכִי, כִּי יְיָ גָּמַל עָלָיְכִי. כִּי חִלַּצְתָּ נַפְשִׁי מִמָּוֶת, אֶת עֵינִי מִן דִּמְעָה, אֶת רַגְלִי מִדֶּחִי. אֶתְהַלֵּךְ לִפְנֵי יְיָ בְּאַרְצוֹת הַחַיִּים. הֶאֱמַנְתִּי כִּי אֲדַבֵּר, אֲנִי עָנִיתִי מְאֹד. אֲנִי אָמַרְתִּי בְחָפְזִי: כָּל הָאָדָם כֹּזֵב.

מָה אָשִׁיב

לַיְיָ כָּל תַּגְמוּלוֹהִי עָלָי. כּוֹס יְשׁוּעוֹת אֶשָּׂא וּבְשֵׁם יְיָ אֶקְרָא. נְדָרַי לַיְיָ אֲשַׁלֵּם נֶגְדָה נָּא לְכָל עַמּוֹ. יָקָר בְּעֵינֵי יְיָ הַמָּוְתָה לַחֲסִידָיו. אָנָּה, יְיָ, כִּי אֲנִי עַבְדֶּךָ, אֲנִי עַבְדְּךָ בֶּן אֲמָתֶךָ, פִּתַּחְתָּ לְמוֹסֵרָי. לְךָ אֶזְבַּח זֶבַח תּוֹדָה וּבְשֵׁם יְיָ אֶקְרָא. נְדָרַי לַיְיָ אֲשַׁלֵּם נֶגְדָה נָּא לְכָל עַמּוֹ. בְּחַצְרוֹת בֵּית יְיָ בְּתוֹכֵכִי יְרוּשָׁלָםִ, הַלְלוּיָהּ. (תְּהִלִּים קטז)

הַלְלוּ אֶת יְיָ, כָּל גּוֹיִם, שַׁבְּחוּהוּ, כָּל הָאֻמִּים. כִּי גָבַר עָלֵינוּ חַסְדּוֹ, וֶאֱמֶת יְיָ לְעוֹלָם, הַלְלוּיָהּ. (תְּהִלִּים קיז)

A Handful of Honey

Rabbi Yochanan said:
I recall that when an infant broke open a piece of carob, a stream of honey would streak both of his arms.

(Baba Batra, XCI, B)

A Land Flowing with Milk & Honey

It is told of Rabbi Yonathan ben Elazar, who was sitting under a fig tree one summer night, and the fig tree was loaded with lovely figs. The dew came, and those very same figs absorbed honey and fell down to the ground. And the wind mixed them with the dust, and a she goat came and dripped her milk into the honey, and the milk combined with the honey.

Rabbi Yonathan called to his pupils and told them: Come and see an example of the world to come.

(Midrash Tankhuma, Titzaveh, XXIII)

Psalm 118: O GIVE THANKS UNTO THE LORD;
for He is good; for His lovingkindness endures for ever.
O let Israel say, that His lovingkindness endures for ever.
O let the house of Aaron say, that His lovingkindness endures for ever.
O let them that fear the Lord say, that His lovingkindness endures for ever.

Out of my straits I called upon the Lord; the Lord answered me by setting me free. The Lord is for me, I will not fear; what can man do unto me? The Lord is for me among those that help me; I shall therefore see my desire on them that hate me. It is better to trust in the Lord than to confide in man. It is better to trust in the Lord than to confide in princes. All nations surrounded me; in the Name of the Lord I cut them down. They surrounded me like bees – they were extinguished as a fire of thorns – in the Name of the Lord I cut them down. You thrust at me that I might fall; but the Lord helped me. The Lord is my strength and song; and He is my salvation. The voice of exulting and salvation is in the tents of the righteous; the right hand of the Lord does valiantly. The right hand of the Lord is exalted; the right hand of the Lord does valiantly. I shall not die but live, and recount the works of the Lord. The Lord has chastened me; but He has not given me over unto death. Open to me the gates of righteousness; I will give thanks unto the Lord. This is the gate of the Lord; the righteous may enter into it.

From this verse onwards, each verse is recited twice.

I WILL GIVE THANKS UNTO YOU, for You have answered unto me, and are my salvation. The stone which the builders rejected became the headstone of the corner. This was the Lord's doing; it is marvelous in our eyes. This is the day which the Lord has made; we will be glad and rejoice on it.

Save, we beseech You, O Lord. Save, we beseech You, O Lord.

Send prosperity, we beseech You, O Lord. Send prosperity, we beseech You, O Lord.

Blessed be he that comes in the Name of the Lord; we bless you out of the house of the Lord. The Lord is God, He hath given us light; bind the festive offerings to the horns of the altar with cords. You are my God, and I will give thanks unto You; You are my God, I will exalt You, O give thanks unto the Lord, for he is good; for His lovingkindness endures for ever.

הוֹדוּ לַיְיָ כִּי טוֹב, כִּי לְעוֹלָם חַסְדּוֹ יֹאמַר נָא יִשְׂרָאֵל כִּי לְעוֹלָם חַסְדּוֹ יֹאמְרוּ נָא בֵית אַהֲרֹן כִּי לְעוֹלָם חַסְדּוֹ יֹאמְרוּ נָא
יִרְאֵי יְיָ כִּי לְעוֹלָם חַסְדּוֹ

מִן הַמֵּצַר

קָרָאתִי יָּה, עָנָנִי בַמֶּרְחָב יָּה. יְיָ לִי לֹא אִירָא, מַה יַּעֲשֶׂה לִי אָדָם? יְיָ לִי בְּעֹזְרָי, וַאֲנִי אֶרְאֶה בְשֹׂנְאָי. טוֹב לַחֲסוֹת בַּיְיָ מִבְּטֹחַ בָּאָדָם. טוֹב לַחֲסוֹת בַּיְיָ מִבְּטֹחַ בִּנְדִיבִים. כָּל גּוֹיִם סְבָבוּנִי, בְּשֵׁם יְיָ כִּי אֲמִילַם. סַבּוּנִי גַם סְבָבוּנִי, בְּשֵׁם יְיָ כִּי אֲמִילַם. סַבּוּנִי כִדְבוֹרִים, דֹּעֲכוּ כְּאֵשׁ קוֹצִים, בְּשֵׁם יְיָ כִּי אֲמִילַם. דָּחֹה דְחִיתַנִי לִנְפֹּל, וַיְיָ עֲזָרָנִי. עָזִּי וְזִמְרָת יָהּ, וַיְהִי לִי לִישׁוּעָה. קוֹל רִנָּה וִישׁוּעָה בְּאָהֳלֵי צַדִּיקִים, יְמִין יְיָ עֹשָׂה חָיִל. יְמִין יְיָ רוֹמֵמָה, יְמִין יְיָ עֹשָׂה חָיִל. לֹא אָמוּת, כִּי אֶחְיֶה וַאֲסַפֵּר מַעֲשֵׂי יָהּ, יַסֹּר יִסְּרַנִּי יָּהּ, וְלַמָּוֶת לֹא נְתָנָנִי. פִּתְחוּ לִי שַׁעֲרֵי צֶדֶק, אָבֹא בָם אוֹדֶה יָּהּ. זֶה הַשַּׁעַר לַיְיָ, צַדִּיקִים יָבֹאוּ בוֹ.

Redemption

When the Lord brought back those who returned to Zion
We were like dreamers.
Then our mouth was filled with laughter,
Our tongue with songs of joy.
Then, among the nations it was said:
The Lord has done great things for them.
The Lord has done great things for us;
We were glad.
Restore us to what we were, Lord,
Like the streams of water in the Negev Desert.
May those who sow tearfully
Reap with songs of joy,
Coming with songs of joy as he bears his sheaves.

(Psalms CXXVI)

All Your works shall praise You, O Lord our God; and Your pious ones, the just who do Your will, and all the house of Israel shall thank and bless and praise and glorify and exalt and reverence and sanctify and ascribe sovereignty to Your Name, O our King, in song. For it is good to give thanks unto You, and becoming to sing praises to Your Name. For from everlasting unto everlasting You are God.

Psalm 136: O GIVE THANKS UNTO THE LORD;

for He is good;
for His lovingkindness endures for ever.
O give thanks unto the God of gods;
for His lovingkindness endures for ever.
O give thanks unto the Lord of Lords;
for His lovingkindness endures for ever.
To Him who alone does great marvels;
for His lovingkindness endures for ever.
To Him that by understanding made the heavens;
for His lovingkindness endures for ever.
To Him that spread forth the earth above the waters;
for His lovingkindness endures for ever.
To Him that made great lights;
for His lovingkindness endures for ever.
The sun to rule by day;
for His lovingkindness endures for ever.
The moon and the stars to rule by night;
for His lovingkindness endures for ever.
To Him that smote the Egyptians in their first-born;
for His lovingkindness endures for ever.
And brought out Israel from among them;
for His lovingkindness endures for ever.
With a strong hand and an outstretched arm;
For His lovingkindness endures for ever.
To Him who parted the Red Sea asunder;
for His lovingkindness endures for ever.
And made Israel to pass through the midst of it;
for His lovingkindness endures for ever.
But overthrew Pharaoh and his host in the Red Sea;
for His lovingkindness endures for ever.
To Him who led his people through the wilderness;
for His lovingkindness endures for ever.
To Him who smote great kings;
for His lovingkindness endures for ever.
And slew mighty kings;
for His lovingkindness endures for ever.
Sihon king of the Amorites;
for His lovingkindness endures for ever.
And Og king of Bashan;
for His lovingkindness endures for ever.
And gave their land for a heritage;
for His lovingkindness endures for ever.

מִפָּסוּק זֶה וְאֵילָךְ חוֹזְרִים עַל כָּל פָּסוּק וּפָסוּק פַּעֲמַיִם.

אוֹדְךָ כִּי עֲנִיתָנִי, וַתְּהִי לִי לִישׁוּעָה. אוֹדְךָ.

אֶבֶן מָאֲסוּ הַבּוֹנִים, הָיְתָה לְרֹאשׁ פִּנָּה. אֶבֶן.

מֵאֵת יְיָ הָיְתָה זֹּאת, הִיא נִפְלָאת בְּעֵינֵינוּ. מֵאֵת.

זֶה הַיּוֹם עָשָׂה יְיָ, נָגִילָה וְנִשְׂמְחָה בוֹ. זֶה.

אָנָּא, יְיָ, הוֹשִׁיעָה נָּא!   אָנָּא, יְיָ, הַצְלִיחָה נָּא!
אָנָּא, יְיָ, הוֹשִׁיעָה נָּא!   אָנָּא, יְיָ, הַצְלִיחָה נָּא!

תהלים קי"ח, א-כה

בָּרוּךְ

הַבָּא בְּשֵׁם יְיָ בֵּרַכְנוּכֶם מִבֵּית יְיָ. בָּרוּךְ.

אֵל יְיָ וַיָּאֶר לָנוּ, אִסְרוּ חַג בַּעֲבֹתִים
עַד קַרְנוֹת הַמִּזְבֵּחַ. אֵל.

אֵלִי אַתָּה וְאוֹדֶךָּ אֱלֹהַי – אֲרוֹמְמֶךָּ. אֵלִי.

הוֹדוּ לַיְיָ כִּי טוֹב, כִּי לְעוֹלָם חַסְדּוֹ. הוֹדוּ.

(תְּהִלִּים קי"ח, כו-כט)

הוֹדוּ לַיְיָ כִּי טוֹב,   כִּי לְעוֹלָם חַסְדּוֹ.
הוֹדוּ לֵאלֹהֵי הָאֱלֹהִים,   כִּי לְעוֹלָם חַסְדּוֹ.
הוֹדוּ לַאֲדֹנֵי הָאֲדֹנִים,   כִּי לְעוֹלָם חַסְדּוֹ.
לְעֹשֵׂה נִפְלָאוֹת גְּדֹלוֹת לְבַדּוֹ,   כִּי לְעוֹלָם חַסְדּוֹ.
לְעֹשֵׂה הַשָּׁמַיִם בִּתְבוּנָה,   כִּי לְעוֹלָם חַסְדּוֹ.
לְרוֹקַע הָאָרֶץ עַל הַמָּיִם,   כִּי לְעוֹלָם חַסְדּוֹ.
לְעֹשֵׂה אוֹרִים גְּדֹלִים,   כִּי לְעוֹלָם חַסְדּוֹ.
אֶת הַשֶּׁמֶשׁ לְמֶמְשֶׁלֶת בַּיּוֹם,   כִּי לְעוֹלָם חַסְדּוֹ.
אֶת הַיָּרֵחַ וְכוֹכָבִים לְמֶמְשְׁלוֹת בַּלָּיְלָה,
כִּי לְעוֹלָם חַסְדּוֹ.
לְמַכֵּה מִצְרַיִם בִּבְכוֹרֵיהֶם,   כִּי לְעוֹלָם חַסְדּוֹ.
וַיּוֹצֵא יִשְׂרָאֵל מִתּוֹכָם,   כִּי לְעוֹלָם חַסְדּוֹ.
בְּיָד חֲזָקָה וּבִזְרוֹעַ נְטוּיָה,   כִּי לְעוֹלָם חַסְדּוֹ:
לְגֹזֵר יַם-סוּף לִגְזָרִים,   כִּי לְעוֹלָם חַסְדּוֹ.
וְהֶעֱבִיר יִשְׂרָאֵל בְּתוֹכוֹ,   כִּי לְעוֹלָם חַסְדּוֹ.
וְנִעֵר פַּרְעֹה וְחֵילוֹ בְיַם-סוּף,   כִּי לְעוֹלָם חַסְדּוֹ.
לְמוֹלִיךְ עַמּוֹ בַּמִּדְבָּר,   כִּי לְעוֹלָם חַסְדּוֹ.
לְמַכֵּה מְלָכִים גְּדֹלִים,   כִּי לְעוֹלָם חַסְדּוֹ.
וַיַּהֲרֹג מְלָכִים אַדִּירִים,   כִּי לְעוֹלָם חַסְדּוֹ.
לְסִיחוֹן מֶלֶךְ הָאֱמֹרִי,   כִּי לְעוֹלָם חַסְדּוֹ.
וּלְעוֹג מֶלֶךְ הַבָּשָׁן,   כִּי לְעוֹלָם חַסְדּוֹ.
וְנָתַן אַרְצָם לְנַחֲלָה,   כִּי לְעוֹלָם חַסְדּוֹ.
נַחֲלָה לְיִשְׂרָאֵל עַבְדּוֹ,   כִּי לְעוֹלָם חַסְדּוֹ.

Carob Trees in the Land of Israel

Rabbi Haninah said:
When I came up [to the Land of Israel] from the Diaspora, I undid my belt and that of my son and that of my ox, in order to encircle the girth of a particular carob tree — and I couldn't.

(Jerusalem Talmud, Pe'ah, LXXXVII, Halacha C)

Even a heritage unto Israel His servant;
for His lovingkindness endures for ever.
Who remembered us in our low estate;
for His lovingkindness endures for ever.
And has released us from our adversaries;
for His lovingkindness endures for ever.

He gives food to all flesh;
for His lovingkindness endures for ever.
O give thanks unto the God of heaven;
for His lovingkindness endures for ever.

THE BREATH OF ALL THAT LIVES

shall praise Your Name, O Lord our God, and the spirit of all flesh shall glorify and exalt Your remembrance, O our King. Continually, from eternity to eternity, You are God, and beside You we have no King who redeems and saves, delivers and protects, sustains and pities in all time of trouble and stress; we have no King but You. You are God of the first and of the last; God of all creatures, Lord of all generations, who is lauded with many praises, and who guides His world with lovingkindness and His creatures with mercy. For the Lord neither slumbers nor sleeps; He awakens those that sleep and arouses those that slumber, gives speech to the dumb, loosens the bound, supports the falling, and raises up the bowed. To You we give our thanks.

נָתַן לֶחֶם לְכָל בָּשָׂר, כִּי לְעוֹלָם חַסְדּוֹ.   שֶׁבְּשִׁפְלֵנוּ זָכַר לָנוּ, כִּי לְעוֹלָם חַסְדּוֹ.

הוֹדוּ לְאֵל הַשָּׁמָיִם, כִּי לְעוֹלָם חַסְדּוֹ.   וַיִּפְרְקֵנוּ מִצָּרֵינוּ, כִּי לְעוֹלָם חַסְדּוֹ.

(תְּהִלִּים קלו)

נִשְׁמַת כָּל חַי

תְּבָרֵךְ אֶת שִׁמְךָ יְיָ אֱלֹהֵינוּ, וְרוּחַ כָּל בָּשָׂר תְּפָאֵר וּתְרוֹמֵם זִכְרְךָ, מַלְכֵּנוּ, תָּמִיד. מִן הָעוֹלָם וְעַד הָעוֹלָם אַתָּה אֵל, וּמִבַּלְעָדֶיךָ אֵין לָנוּ מֶלֶךְ, גּוֹאֵל וּמוֹשִׁיעַ, פּוֹדֶה וּמַצִּיל וּמְפַרְנֵס וּמְרַחֵם בְּכָל עֵת צָרָה וְצוּקָה. אֵין לָנוּ מֶלֶךְ אֶלָּא אָתָּה. אֱלֹהֵי הָרִאשׁוֹנִים וְהָאַחֲרוֹנִים, אֱלוֹהַּ כָּל בְּרִיּוֹת, אֲדוֹן כָּל תּוֹלָדוֹת, הַמְהֻלָּל בְּרֹב הַתִּשְׁבָּחוֹת, הַמְנַהֵג עוֹלָמוֹ בְּחֶסֶד וּבְרִיּוֹתָיו בְּרַחֲמִים. וַיְיָ לֹא יָנוּם וְלֹא יִישָׁן, הַמְעוֹרֵר יְשֵׁנִים וְהַמֵּקִיץ נִרְדָּמִים, וְהַמֵּשִׂיחַ אִלְּמִים, וְהַמַּתִּיר אֲסוּרִים, וְהַסּוֹמֵךְ נוֹפְלִים, וְהַזּוֹקֵף כְּפוּפִים, לְךָ לְבַדְּךָ אֲנַחְנוּ מוֹדִים.

אִלּוּ פִינוּ מָלֵא שִׁירָה כַיָּם, וּלְשׁוֹנֵנוּ רִנָּה כַּהֲמוֹן גַּלָּיו, וְשִׂפְתוֹתֵינוּ שֶׁבַח כְּמֶרְחֲבֵי רָקִיעַ, וְעֵינֵינוּ מְאִירוֹת כַּשֶּׁמֶשׁ וְכַיָּרֵחַ, וְיָדֵינוּ פְרוּשׂוֹת כְּנִשְׁרֵי שָׁמָיִם, וְרַגְלֵינוּ קַלּוֹת כָּאַיָּלוֹת – אֵין אֲנַחְנוּ מַסְפִּיקִים לְהוֹדוֹת לְךָ, יְיָ אֱלֹהֵינוּ וֵאלֹהֵי אֲבוֹתֵינוּ, וּלְבָרֵךְ אֶת שְׁמֶךָ, עַל אַחַת מֵאָלֶף, אֶלֶף אַלְפֵי אֲלָפִים וְרִבֵּי רְבָבוֹת פְּעָמִים, הַטּוֹבוֹת שֶׁעָשִׂיתָ עִם אֲבוֹתֵינוּ וְעִמָּנוּ:

The Land of Israel — A Bounteous Land

Rabbi Hiya bar Ashi said in the name of Rav:
In the future all the barren trees in the Land of Israel will be loaded with fruit, as it is written:
For every tree bears its fruit; the fig tree and vine give their full yield. (Joel, II, 22)
(Ketuboth, CXII, B)

HE THAT ABIDES

eternally, exalted and holy is His Name. It is written: "Rejoice in the Lord, O righteous, for praise is comely for the upright" *(Ps. 33:1)*.

In the mouths of the upright You shall be praised; with the words of the righteous You shall be blessed; by the tongue of the pious You shall be extolled; and in the inmost being of the holy You shall be hallowed.

AND IN THE ASSEMBLIES

of the multitudes of Your people, the house of Israel, shall Your Name be glorified in song, O our king, in every generation. For such is the duty of all creatures – before You, O Lord our God, and God of our fathers, to thank, praise, laud, glorify, extol, reverence, bless, exalt and adore, above all the words of the songs and praises of David son of Jesse, Your anointed servant.

BE YOUR NAME PRAISED

for ever, O our King; God and King, great and hallowed in Heaven and on earth. For unto You are becoming, O Lord our God, and God of our fathers, song and praise, hymn and psalm, strength and dominion; victory, greatness, and might; praise and glory; holiness and sovereignty; blessing and thanksgiving, from henceforth and for ever.

מִמִּצְרַיִם גְּאַלְתָּנוּ, יְיָ אֱלֹהֵינוּ, וּמִבֵּית עֲבָדִים פְּדִיתָנוּ, בְּרָעָב זַנְתָּנוּ, וּבְשָׂבָע כִּלְכַּלְתָּנוּ, מֵחֶרֶב הִצַּלְתָּנוּ, וּמִדֶּבֶר מִלַּטְתָּנוּ, וּמֵחֳלָיִים רָעִים וְנֶאֱמָנִים דִּלִּיתָנוּ. עַד הֵנָּה עֲזָרוּנוּ רַחֲמֶיךָ וְלֹא עֲזָבוּנוּ חֲסָדֶיךָ, וְאַל תִּטְּשֵׁנוּ, יְיָ אֱלֹהֵינוּ, לָנֶצַח. עַל כֵּן אֵבָרִים שֶׁפִּלַּגְתָּ בָּנוּ, וְרוּחַ וּנְשָׁמָה שֶׁנָּפַחְתָּ בְּאַפֵּנוּ, וְלָשׁוֹן אֲשֶׁר שַׂמְתָּ בְּפִינוּ – הֵן הֵם יוֹדוּ וִיבָרְכוּ, וִישַׁבְּחוּ וִיפָאֲרוּ, וִירוֹמְמוּ וְיַעֲרִיצוּ, וְיַקְדִּישׁוּ וְיַמְלִיכוּ אֶת שִׁמְךָ, מַלְכֵּנוּ, כִּי כָל פֶּה לְךָ יוֹדֶה, וְכָל לָשׁוֹן לְךָ תִשָּׁבַע, וְכָל בֶּרֶךְ לְךָ תִכְרַע, וְכָל קוֹמָה לְפָנֶיךָ תִשְׁתַּחֲוֶה, וְכָל לְבָבוֹת יִירָאוּךָ, וְכָל קֶרֶב וּכְלָיוֹת יְזַמְּרוּ לִשְׁמֶךָ, כַּדָּבָר שֶׁכָּתוּב: כָּל עַצְמֹתַי תֹּאמַרְנָה: יְיָ, מִי כָמוֹךָ: מַצִּיל עָנִי מֵחָזָק מִמֶּנּוּ, וְעָנִי וְאֶבְיוֹן מִגֹּזְלוֹ.

מִי יִדְמֶה לָּךְ וּמִי יִשְׁוֶה לָּךְ וּמִי יַעֲרָךְ לָךְ, הָאֵל הַגָּדוֹל, הַגִּבּוֹר וְהַנּוֹרָא, אֵל עֶלְיוֹן, קֹנֵה שָׁמַיִם וָאָרֶץ. נְהַלֶּלְךָ וּנְשַׁבֵּחֲךָ וּנְפָאֶרְךָ וּנְבָרֵךְ אֶת שֵׁם קָדְשֶׁךָ, כָּאָמוּר לְדָוִד: בָּרְכִי, נַפְשִׁי, אֶת יְיָ וְכָל קְרָבַי – אֶת שֵׁם קָדְשׁוֹ.

הָאֵל

בְּתַעֲצֻמוֹת עֻזֶּךָ, הַגָּדוֹל בִּכְבוֹד שְׁמֶךָ, הַגִּבּוֹר לָנֶצַח וְהַנּוֹרָא בְּנוֹרְאוֹתֶיךָ. הַמֶּלֶךְ הַיּוֹשֵׁב עַל כִּסֵּא רָם וְנִשָּׂא.

שׁוֹכֵן

עַד, מָרוֹם וְקָדוֹשׁ שְׁמוֹ. וְכָתוּב: "רַנְּנוּ צַדִּיקִים בַּיְיָ, לַיְשָׁרִים נָאוָה תְהִלָּה". בְּפִי יְשָׁרִים תִּתְהַלָּל, וּבְדִבְרֵי צַדִּיקִים תִּתְבָּרַךְ, וּבִלְשׁוֹן חֲסִידִים תִּתְרוֹמָם, וּבְקֶרֶב קְדוֹשִׁים תִּתְקַדָּשׁ.

וּבְמַקְהֲלוֹת

רִבְבוֹת עַמְּךָ בֵּית יִשְׂרָאֵל בְּרִנָּה יִתְפָּאֵר שִׁמְךָ, מַלְכֵּנוּ, בְּכָל דּוֹר וָדוֹר, שֶׁכֵּן חוֹבַת כָּל הַיְצוּרִים לְפָנֶיךָ, יְיָ אֱלֹהֵינוּ וֵאלֹהֵי אֲבוֹתֵינוּ, לְהוֹדוֹת, לְהַלֵּל, לְשַׁבֵּחַ, לְפָאֵר, לְרוֹמֵם, לְהַדֵּר, לְבָרֵךְ, לְעַלֵּה וּלְקַלֵּס עַל כָּל דִּבְרֵי שִׁירוֹת וְתִשְׁבְּחוֹת דָּוִד בֶּן יִשַׁי עַבְדֶּךָ, מְשִׁיחֶךָ.

The People of Israel — An Eternal People

Just as a date palm is attractive to look at and all of its fruit is sweet and good,
So the Son of David [the People of Israel] is attractive to look at, and his distinction and all of his deeds are good and sweet....
Just as the roots of the cedar of Lebanon are strong and very deep in the earth, so that even all the winds of the world which come and blow on it cannot move it from its place.
So the strength and deeds of the Son of David are abundant before the Holy One, Blessed Be He,
That even all the enemies which come upon him cannot move him from his place.

(The Chapters of Rabbi Eliezer, Chapter XIX)

BLESSED ARE YOU,

O Lord, God and King, great in praises, God of thanksgivings, Lord of wonders, who delights in songs of praise, King and God, Life of all worlds.

All recite the blessing on the fourth cup, and drink it leaning to the left. Then the Concluding Blessing is recited:

BLESSED ARE YOU

O Lord our God, King of the Universe, Creator of the fruit of the vine.

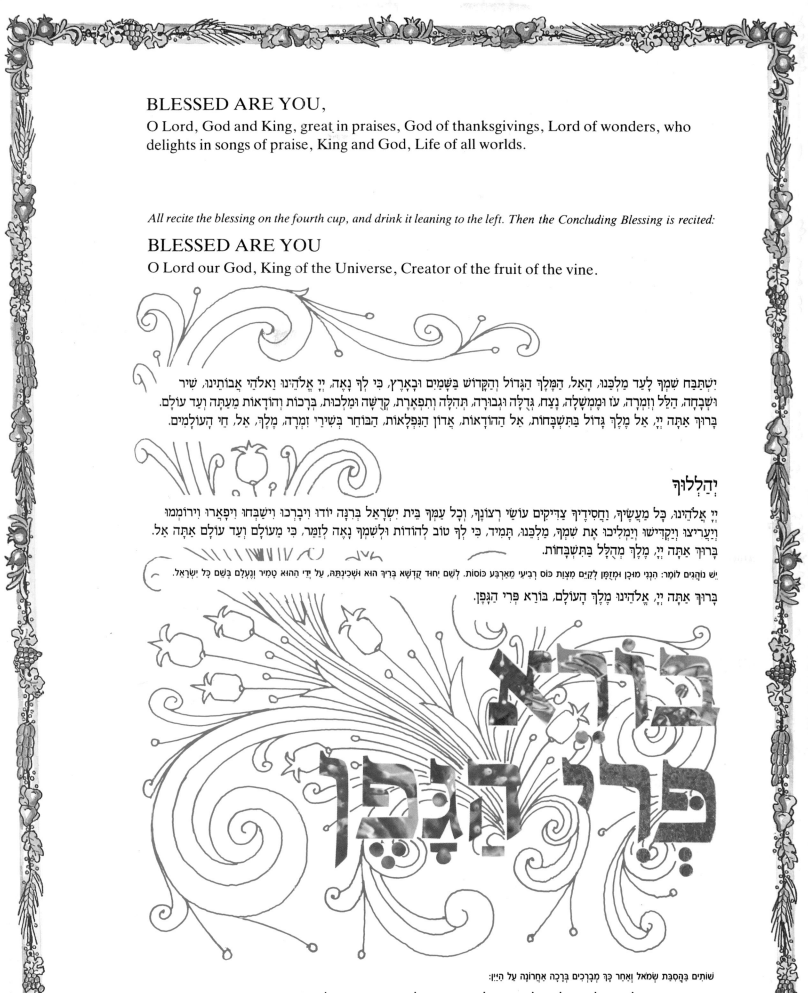

יִשְׁתַּבַּח שִׁמְךָ לָעַד מַלְכֵּנוּ, הָאֵל, הַמֶּלֶךְ הַגָּדוֹל וְהַקָּדוֹשׁ בַּשָּׁמַיִם וּבָאָרֶץ, כִּי לְךָ נָאֶה, יְיָ אֱלֹהֵינוּ וֵאלֹהֵי אֲבוֹתֵינוּ, שִׁיר וּשְׁבָחָה, הַלֵּל וְזִמְרָה, עֹז וּמֶמְשָׁלָה, נֶצַח, גְּדֻלָּה וּגְבוּרָה, תְּהִלָּה וְתִפְאֶרֶת, קְדֻשָּׁה וּמַלְכוּת, בְּרָכוֹת וְהוֹדָאוֹת מֵעַתָּה וְעַד עוֹלָם. בָּרוּךְ אַתָּה יְיָ, אֵל מֶלֶךְ גָּדוֹל בַּתִּשְׁבָּחוֹת, אֵל הַהוֹדָאוֹת, אֲדוֹן הַנִּפְלָאוֹת, הַבּוֹחֵר בְּשִׁירֵי זִמְרָה, מֶלֶךְ, אֵל, חֵי הָעוֹלָמִים.

יְהַלְלוּךָ

יְיָ אֱלֹהֵינוּ, כָּל מַעֲשֶׂיךָ, וַחֲסִידֶיךָ צַדִּיקִים עוֹשֵׂי רְצוֹנֶךָ, וְכָל עַמְּךָ בֵּית יִשְׂרָאֵל בְּרִנָּה יוֹדוּ וִיבָרְכוּ וִישַׁבְּחוּ וִיפָאֲרוּ וִירוֹמְמוּ וְיַעֲרִיצוּ וְיַקְדִּישׁוּ וְיַמְלִיכוּ אֶת שִׁמְךָ, מַלְכֵּנוּ, תָּמִיד, כִּי לְךָ טוֹב לְהוֹדוֹת וּלְשִׁמְךָ נָאֶה לְזַמֵּר, כִּי מֵעוֹלָם וְעַד עוֹלָם אַתָּה אֵל. בָּרוּךְ אַתָּה יְיָ, מֶלֶךְ מְהֻלָּל בַּתִּשְׁבָּחוֹת.

יֵשׁ נוֹהֲגִים לוֹמַר: הִנְנִי מוּכָן וּמְזֻמָּן לְקַיֵּם מִצְוַת כּוֹס רְבִיעִי מֵאַרְבַּע כּוֹסוֹת. לְשֵׁם יִחוּד קֻדְשָׁא בְּרִיךְ הוּא וּשְׁכִינְתֵּהּ, עַל יְדֵי הַהוּא טָמִיר וְנֶעְלָם בְּשֵׁם כָּל יִשְׂרָאֵל.

בָּרוּךְ אַתָּה יְיָ, אֱלֹהֵינוּ מֶלֶךְ הָעוֹלָם, בּוֹרֵא פְּרִי הַגָּפֶן.

שׁוֹתִים בַּהֲסִבַּת שְׂמֹאל וְאַחַר כָּךְ מְבָרְכִים בְּרָכָה אַחֲרוֹנָה עַל הַיַּיִן:

בָּרוּךְ אַתָּה יְיָ, אֱלֹהֵינוּ מֶלֶךְ הָעוֹלָם, עַל הַגֶּפֶן וְעַל פְּרִי הַגֶּפֶן וְעַל תְּנוּבַת הַשָּׂדֶה וְעַל אֶרֶץ חֶמְדָּה טוֹבָה וּרְחָבָה, שֶׁרָצִיתָ וְהִנְחַלְתָּ לַאֲבוֹתֵינוּ לֶאֱכֹל מִפִּרְיָהּ וְלִשְׂבֹּעַ מִטּוּבָהּ.

And it will Come to Pass
at the End of Days

And behold, the days are coming,
says the Lord,
When the ploughman will meet the reaper
And the crusher of grapes, the sower
of seeds; the mountains will drip new wine
and all the hills will be dissolved in it.
And I will return Israel My people to its
former state,
And they will rebuild the ruined cities and
inhabit them,
And plant vineyards and drink their wine,
And make gardens and eat of their fruit.
And I will plant them on their land, and no
more will they be uprooted
from their land....

(Amos, IX, 13-15)

Blessed are You, O Lord our God, King of the Universe, for the vine and for the fruit of the vine, and for the pleasant, goodly, and ample land which You did please to give as an inheritance to our Fathers, to eat of its fruit and to be satisfied with its goodness. Have mercy, O Lord, upon Israel Your people and upon Jerusalem Your city and upon Zion the abode of Your glory and upon Your altar and upon Your shrine. Build Jerusalem the Holy City again speedily in our days; bring us up into its midst and cause us to rejoice in its establishment, so that we may eat of its fruit and be satisfied with its goodness and bless You for it in holiness and purity; (be pleased to strengthen us upon this Sabbath day) and make us rejoice upon this Feast of Matzot, for You, O Lord, are Good, and do good to all; and we shall thank You for the Land and for the fruit of the vine. Blessed are You, O Lord, for the Land and for the fruit of the vine! Accomplished is the order of the Passover according to its precept, in all its law and its custom. Even as we have had the merit to order it, so may we have the merit to fulfill it.

God has already found your doings desirous, if you have followed the order of the Passover Seder.

You Pure One, who dwells on high! Raise up the congregation that is without number! Speedily lead the offshoots of the stock which You have planted, redeemed, to Zion in song.

THE COMING YEAR
IN JERUSALEM!

רַחֵם, יְיָ אֱלֹהֵינוּ, עַל יִשְׂרָאֵל עַמֶּךְ וְעַל יְרוּשָׁלַיִם עִירֶךְ וְעַל צִיּוֹן מִשְׁכַּן כְּבוֹדֶךְ וְעַל מִזְבַּחֶךְ וְעַל הֵיכָלֶךְ, וּבְנֵה יְרוּשָׁלַיִם עִיר הַקֹּדֶשׁ בִּמְהֵרָה בְיָמֵינוּ, וְשַׂמְּחֵנוּ בְּבִנְיָנָהּ, וְנֹאכַל מִפִּרְיָהּ וְנִשְׂבַּע מִטּוּבָהּ, וּנְבָרֶכְךָ עָלֶיהָ בִּקְדֻשָּׁה וּבְטָהֳרָה (בַּשַּׁבָּת אוֹמְרִים: וּרְצֵה וְהַחֲלִיצֵנוּ בְּיוֹם הַשַּׁבָּת הַזֶּה), וְשַׂמְּחֵנוּ בְּיוֹם חַג הַמַּצּוֹת הַזֶּה, כִּי אַתָּה, יְיָ, טוֹב וּמֵטִיב לַכֹּל, וְנוֹדֶה לְּךָ עַל הָאָרֶץ וְעַל פְּרִי הַגָּפֶן. בָּרוּךְ אַתָּה יְיָ, עַל הָאָרֶץ וְעַל פְּרִי הַגָּפֶן.

בָּרוּךְ אַתָּה יְיָ, אֱלֹהֵינוּ מֶלֶךְ הָעוֹלָם, בּוֹרֵא נְפָשׁוֹת רַבּוֹת וְחֶסְרוֹנָן, עַל כָּל מַה שֶּׁבָּרָא לְהַחֲיוֹת בָּהֶם נֶפֶשׁ כָּל חָי. בָּרוּךְ חַי הָעוֹלָמִים.

נִרְצָה

כְּבָר רָצָה הָאֱלֹהִים אֶת מַעֲשֶׂיךָ, אִם עָשִׂיתָ כַּסֵּדֶר הַזֶּה.

חֲסַל סִדּוּר פֶּסַח כְּהִלְכָתוֹ, כְּכָל מִשְׁפָּטוֹ וְחֻקָּתוֹ.

כַּאֲשֶׁר זָכִינוּ לְסַדֵּר אוֹתוֹ, כֵּן נִזְכֶּה לַעֲשׂוֹתוֹ. זָךְ שׁוֹכֵן מְעוֹנָה, קוֹמֵם קְהַל עֲדַת מִי מָנָה; בְּקָרוֹב נַהֵל נִטְעֵי כַנָּה,

פְּדוּיִים לְצִיּוֹן בְּרִנָּה.

The People of Israel & the Torah

Once, an old man asked Eliyahu:
Rabbi, why are the words of the Torah dearer to the Holy One, Blessed Be He than all the inhabitants of the universe?

Eliyahu said: My son, it is because the words of the Torah determine the merits of the People of Israel on the scale of justice and educate them to good deeds....
This may be compared to a king who has many sons and many servants, including one old servant who teaches the king's sons pleasing manners and good deeds.
And each and every day, when the king's sons and servants come before him, he passes over them all, showing preference to the old servant in his household.

The other servants asked him: Why do you love the old servant more than anyone else?
The king said to them: Were it not for the old servant, who teaches my sons good and pleasing manners and good deeds, what would become of them?
So is it regarding the words of the Torah: They are dear to Me, since they determine the merits of the People of Israel on the scale of justice and educate them to good deeds — dearer than all the inhabitants of the universe and everything I have created.

(Tana Rabbi Eliyahu, XIV)

לְשָׁנָה הַבָּאָה בִּירוּשָׁלַיִם הַבְּנוּיָה.

On the second day of Passover, the "counting of the Omer" is begun.

לְמָחֳרַת הַפֶּסַח מַתְחִילִים לִסְפֹּר אֶת סְפִירַת הָעֹמֶר.

סְפִירַת הָעֹמֶר

בָּרוּךְ אַתָּה יְיָ, אֱלֹהֵינוּ מֶלֶךְ הָעוֹלָם, אֲשֶׁר קִדְּשָׁנוּ בְּמִצְוֹתָיו וְצִוָּנוּ עַל סְפִירַת הָעֹמֶר.

הַיּוֹם יוֹם אֶחָד לָעֹמֶר.

The People of Israel are Compared to a King's Daughter

A comparison may be made to a king's daughter who was gathering up the gleanings of a field. The king happened by and recognized that this was his daughter. He despatched his devotee, who took her and sat her down with the king in his coach.

Then her friends were amazed, and said to her: Only yesterday you were gathering gleanings, and today you sit in the king's coach.

She replied: I'm just as amazed at myself as you are....

So it was when the People of Israel were enslaved in Egypt, hard at work with clay and bricks, despised and downcast in the eyes of the Egyptians. And when they became free men and were redeemed and were made deputies over all of humanity, the nations of the world were amazed and said: Only yesterday you were working with clay and bricks, and now you're free men?

And the People of Israel said to them, just as you are amazed, so are we.

(Shir Hashirim [Song of Songs] Raba, VI)

AND IT HAPPENED AT THE MIDDLE OF THE NIGHT

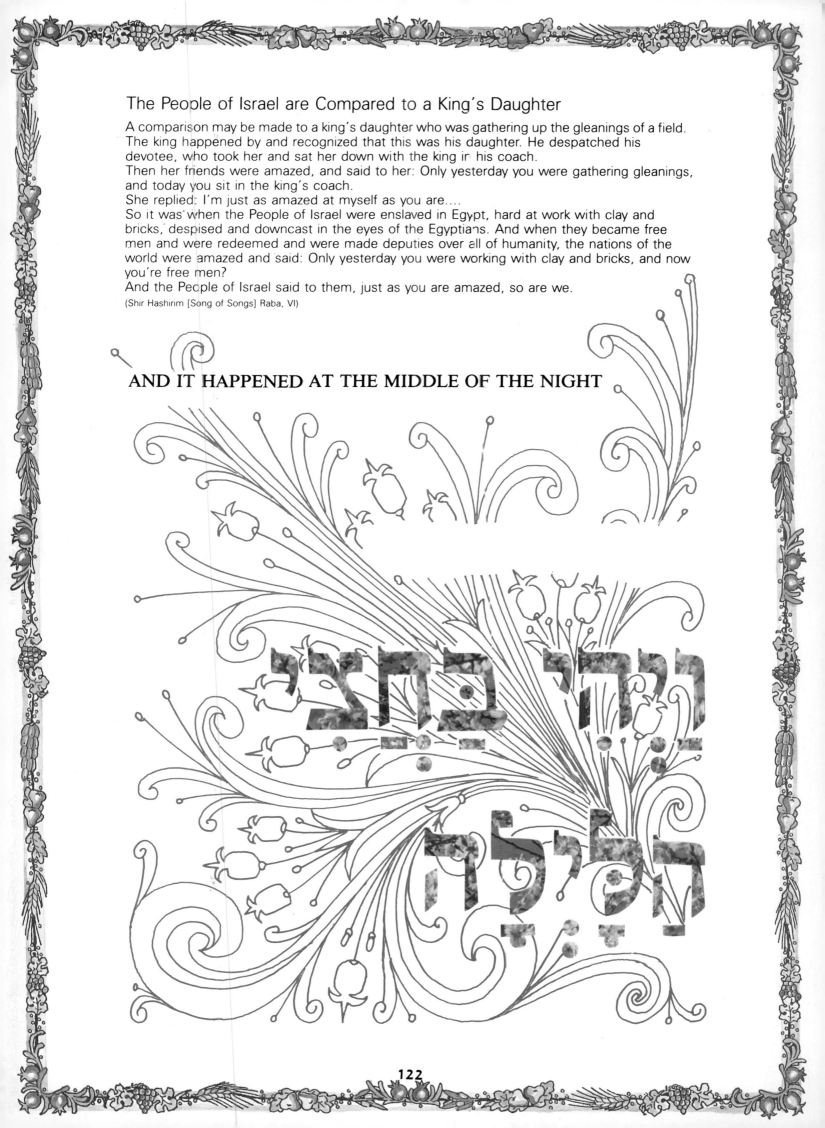

ויהי בחצי הלילה

On the first night the following is recited:

AND IT HAPPENED AT THE MIDDLE OF THE NIGHT

(Ex. XII, 29)

Of old, Thou didst perform most
miracles at night,
At the beginning of the watches
of this night.
The righteous proselyte prevailed
when he broke up his
host at night *(Gen. XIV, 15)*
And it happened at the middle
of the night,

Thou didst judge the king of Gerar
in a dream of night *(Gen. XX, 3)*,
The Syrian was struck with terror
'yesternight' *(Gen. XXXI, 24)*
And Israel strove with God,
and yet prevailed at night.
(Gen. XXXII, 23-7)
And it happened at the middle
of the night.

The first-born seed of Pathros didst
Thou crush in
dead of night *(Ex. XII, 29)*.
Their substance they found not
when they rose at night.
The battalions of Harosheth's
captain didst sweep away through
the stars of night *(Jud. V, 20)*
And it happened at the middle
of the night.

The impious thought to scatter
My chosen.
Thou didst shame his dead
by night *(II Kings XIX, 35)*.

Bel and his pillar were prostrate
at night *(Dan. II, 34)*.
The man of delight was told the key
of mysteries of night. *(Dan. II, 19)*
And it happened at the middle
of the night.

He who was drunken in the sacred
vessels–he was
slain that night,
When he who had escaped the lions'
den revealed the awesome
dream of night *(Dan. V, 30)*.
The Agagite cherished hatred, and
missives wrote at night. *(Est. IV, 12)*
And it happened at the middle
of the night.

Thou didst arouse Thy victory on
him, when sleep fled
at night *(Est. VI, 1)*.
The wine-press Thou shalt tread for
him who asks the watchman,
What of night? *(Is. LXIII, 3; XXI, 11)*
Like a watchman shall He answer,
saying: 'Morning's come, and,
too, the night.'
And it happened at the middle
of the night.

Bring near the day, which
is not day nor night!
All-High! Make known that Thine
is day and Thine is night!
Set guards about Thy city, all the
day and all the night:
Make Thou light as the day
the dark of night!
And it happened at the middle
of the night.

בְּלֵיל רִאשׁוֹן אוֹמְרִים:

וּבְכֵן וַיְהִי בַּחֲצִי הַלָּיְלָה.

אָז רֹב נִסִּים הִפְלֵאתָ בַּלַּיְלָה,
בְּרֹאשׁ אַשְׁמוּרוֹת זֶה הַלַּיְלָה,
גֵּר צֶדֶק נִצַּחְתּוֹ כְּנֶחֱלַק לוֹ לַיְלָה,
וַיְהִי בַּחֲצִי הַלָּיְלָה.

דַּנְתָּ מֶלֶךְ גְּרָר בַּחֲלוֹם הַלַּיְלָה,
הִפְחַדְתָּ אֲרַמִּי בְּאֶמֶשׁ לַיְלָה,
וַיָּשַׂר יִשְׂרָאֵל לַמַּלְאָךְ וַיּוּכַל לוֹ לַיְלָה,
וַיְהִי בַּחֲצִי הַלָּיְלָה.

זֶרַע בְּכוֹרֵי פַתְרוֹס מָחַצְתָּ בַּחֲצִי הַלַּיְלָה,
חֵילָם לֹא מָצְאוּ בְּקוּמָם בַּלַּיְלָה,
טִיסַת נְגִיד חֲרֹשֶׁת סִלִּיתָ בְּכוֹכְבֵי לַיְלָה,
וַיְהִי בַּחֲצִי הַלָּיְלָה.

יָעַץ מְחָרֵף לְנוֹפֵף אִוּוּי – הוֹבַשְׁתָּ פְגָרָיו בַּלַּיְלָה,
כָּרַע בֵּל וּמַצָּבוֹ בְּאִישׁוֹן לַיְלָה,

לְאִישׁ חֲמוּדוֹת נִגְלָה רָז חֲזוֹת לַיְלָה,
וַיְהִי בַּחֲצִי הַלַּיְלָה.

מִשְׁתַּכֵּר בִּכְלֵי קֹדֶשׁ נֶהֱרַג בּוֹ בַּלַּיְלָה,
נוֹשַׁע מִבּוֹר אֲרָיוֹת פּוֹתֵר בְּעִתּוּתֵי לַיְלָה,
שִׂנְאָה נָטַר אֲגָגִי וְכָתַב סְפָרִים בַּלַּיְלָה,
וַיְהִי בַּחֲצִי הַלַּיְלָה.

עוֹרַרְתָּ נִצְחֲךָ עָלָיו בְּנֶדֶד שְׁנַת לַיְלָה,
פּוּרָה תִדְרוֹךְ לְשׁוֹמֵר מַה מִלַּיְלָה,
צָרַח כַּשּׁוֹמֵר וְשָׂח אָתָא בֹקֶר וְגַם לַיְלָה,
וַיְהִי בַּחֲצִי הַלַּיְלָה.

קָרֵב יוֹם, אֲשֶׁר הוּא לֹא יוֹם וְלֹא לַיְלָה,
רָם הוֹדַע, כִּי לְךָ הַיּוֹם אַף לְךָ הַלַּיְלָה,
שׁוֹמְרִים הַפְקֵד לְעִירְךָ כָּל הַיּוֹם וְכָל הַלַּיְלָה,
תָּאִיר כְּאוֹר יוֹם חֶשְׁכַת לַיְלָה,
וַיְהִי בַּחֲצִי הַלָּיְלָה.

The Land of Israel is Blessed with Oil

"And he will bathe his feet in oil." (Deuteronomy XXXIII, 24) This teaches us that the land of [the tribe of] Asher overflows with oil like a fountain.

Once the people of Ladocia found themselves in need of oil. They appointed a delegate and said to him: Go and buy us oil for 100 ribo.

He went to Jerusalem and told the people there: I need 100 ribo worth of oil.

They told him: Go to Gush Halav.

He went to Gush Halav and said to the people there: I need 100 ribo worth of oil.

They said to him: Go to that man. He went to that man's house and asked for him, but didn't find him.

People said: He's in the field. Then the delegate went and found the man hoeing under an olive tree.

The delegate said: Could it be that this man really has 100 ribo worth of oil? It seems as though the Jews were making fun of me.

When they arrived at his house, the man called out to his maid: Come and wash our feet. She filled a cup with oil and washed their feet for them.

The man then broke bread with his visitor, and he ate and drank. After eating and drinking the man stood up and measured out 100 ribo worth of oil. He said to the visitor: Do you want more?

He answered: I have no more money.

He said to him: Take it, and I'll come with you and get my money.

And he measured out 18 ribo worth of oil for him.

They said: There is not a single donkey or a camel in the entire Land of Israel which has not carried off this man's oil.

When they reached his city, the residents came out to praise the delegate.

He said to them: Do not offer up such praise [to me], but to this man; everything belongs to him.

And what's more, I owe him 18 ribo.

(Yalkut Shimoni to Vezoth Habracha, XXXIII)

On the second night the following is recited:

AND YE SHALL SAY, 'TIS THE OFFERING OF THE PASSOVER'
(Ex. XII, 27)

בְּלֵיל שֵׁנִי אוֹמְרִים:

אֹמֶץ גְּבוּרוֹתֶיךָ הִפְלֵאתָ בַּפֶּסַח,

בְּרֹאשׁ כָּל מוֹעֲדוֹת נִשֵּׂאתָ פֶּסַח,

גִּלִּיתָ לְאֶזְרָחִי חֲצוֹת לֵיל פֶּסַח,

וַאֲמַרְתֶּם זֶבַח פֶּסַח.

דְּלָתָיו דָּפַקְתָּ כְּחֹם הַיּוֹם בַּפֶּסַח,

הִסְעִיד נוֹצְצִים עֻגוֹת מַצּוֹת בַּפֶּסַח,

וְאֶל הַבָּקָר רָץ זֵכֶר לְשׁוֹר עֵרֶךְ פֶּסַח,

וַאֲמַרְתֶּם זֶבַח פֶּסַח.

זֹעֲמוּ סְדוֹמִים וְלֹהֲטוּ בָאֵשׁ בַּפֶּסַח,

חֻלַּץ לוֹט מֵהֶם וּמַצּוֹת אָפָה בְּקֵץ פֶּסַח,

טִאטֵאתָ אַדְמַת מֹף וְנֹף בְּעָבְרְךָ בַּפֶּסַח,

וַאֲמַרְתֶּם זֶבַח פֶּסַח.

יָהּ, רֹאשׁ כָּל אוֹן מָחַצְתָּ בְּלֵיל שִׁמּוּר פֶּסַח,

כַּבִּיר, עַל בֵּן בְּכוֹר פָּסַחְתָּ בְּדַם פֶּסַח,

לְבִלְתִּי תֵּת מַשְׁחִית לָבֹא בִּפְתָחַי בַּפֶּסַח,

וַאֲמַרְתֶּם זֶבַח פֶּסַח.

מְסֻגֶּרֶת סֻגְּרָה בְּעִתּוֹתֵי פֶּסַח,

נִשְׁמְדָה מִדְיָן בִּצְלִיל שְׂעוֹרֵי עֹמֶר פֶּסַח,

שֹׂרְפוּ מִשְׁמַנֵּי פּוּל וְלוּד בִּיקַד יְקוֹד פֶּסַח,

וַאֲמַרְתֶּם זֶבַח פֶּסַח.

עוֹד הַיּוֹם בְּנֹב לַעֲמֹד עַד גָּעָה עוֹנַת פֶּסַח,

פַּס יָד כָּתְבָה לְקַעֲקֵעַ צוּל בַּפֶּסַח,

צָפֹה הַצָּפִית עָרֹךְ הַשֻּׁלְחָן בַּפֶּסַח,

וַאֲמַרְתֶּם זֶבַח פֶּסַח.

קָהָל כִּנְּסָה הֲדַסָּה לְשַׁלֵּשׁ צוֹם בַּפֶּסַח,

רֹאשׁ מִבֵּית רָשָׁע מָחַצְתָּ בְּעֵץ חֲמִשִּׁים בַּפֶּסַח,

שְׁתֵּי אֵלֶּה רֶגַע תָּבִיא לְעוּצִית בַּפֶּסַח,

תָּעֹז יָדְךָ, תָּרוּם יְמִינֶךָ כְּלֵיל הִתְקַדֵּשׁ חַג הַפֶּסַח,

וַאֲמַרְתֶּם זֶבַח פֶּסַח.

The strength of Thy might was wondrously displayed on Passover:
Above all feasts didst Thou raise up the Passover:
To the Ezrahite Thou didst reveal the midnight marvels
of the Passover. *(Ps. LXXXIX, 1)*
And ye shall say, 'Tis the offering of the Passover.'

Upon his doors didst knock at noontide heat on Passover:
He feasted angels with unleavened cakes on Passover *(Gen. XVIII)*:
'And to the herd he ran': so do we read the Lesson
of the Ox on Passover,
(Lev. XXII, 26-XXIII, 44)
And ye shall say, 'Tis the offering of the Passover.'

The furious Sodomites didst Thou consume in fire on Passover:
Lot, saved from them, baked unleavened bread towards
the end of Passover *(Gen. XIX)*:
Thou didst sweep clean the land of Moph and Noph when Thou didst near on Passover.
And ye shall say, 'Tis the offering of the Passover.'

Lord! Thou didst smite each first-born's head on Passover:
Omnipotent! Thy first-born didst Thou spare on Passover:
Not suffering a destroyer to pass my doors on Passover. *(Ex. XII).*

The Quality of the People of Israel

This nation is compared to both dust and the stars.
When they backslide — they backslide as low as dust,
And when they exalt themselves — it is to the stars.

(Megillah, XVI, A)

And ye shall say, 'Tis the offering of the Passover.'

Strong Jericho was straitly closed towards the time
of Passover *(Josh. VI)*:
Midian was destroyed by a cake of barley, the offering
of the Passover *(Jud. VII)*:
The mighty ones of Pul and Lud were burned up in a conflagration
on the Passover. *(IS. LXVI, 19)*.
And ye shall say, 'Tis the offering of the Passover.'

Destined was he to stay in Nob, until three came
the time of Passover *(Is. X, 32)*:
A Hand wrote Babylon's fate upon the wall on Passover *(Dan. V, 24)*:

'The watch is set: the table spread'–on Passover. *(Is. XXI, 5)*
And ye shall say, 'Tis the offering of the Passover.'

Hadassah gathered all, for three-fold fast on Passover *(Est. IV, 16)*
Thou didst smite the chief of the evil house on Passover *(Est. VII, 9)*
'These twain' shalt Thou together bring for Edom
on the Passover *(Is. XLVII, 9)*:
Thy hand shall be strong: Thy right arm uplifted as on the night
of sanctification of the Passover
And ye shall say, 'Tis the offering of the Passover.'

TO HIM IS IT BECOMING, TO HIM SHALL IT BECOME!

Mighty in kingship, Chosen of right!
To Him say His armies:
'To Thee, and to Thee,
To Thee, yea to
Thee, To Thee, true, to Thee,
To Thee, Lord, is the sovereignty:
To Him is it becoming,
to Him shall it become!

כִּי לוֹ נָאֶה,
כִּי לוֹ יָאֶה.

אַדִּיר בִּמְלוּכָה, בָּחוּר כַּהֲלָכָה, גְּדוּדָיו יֹאמְרוּ לוֹ:
לְךָ וּלְךָ, לְךָ כִּי לְךָ, לְךָ אַף לְךָ,
לְךָ יְיָ הַמַּמְלָכָה,
כִּי לוֹ נָאֶה, כִּי לוֹ יָאֶה.

The People of Israel are Compared to an Apple Tree

Why are the People of Israel compared to an apple tree? This is to teach you:
Just as with an apple tree, its fruit appears before its leaves do,
So the People of Israel – who placed We will do, before We will hear.

(Shabbath, LXXXVIII, A)

The People of Israel are Compared to a Nut

Just as with nuts, when you take one from the pile, the rest roll away one after another,
So it is with the People of Israel, when one of them is taken away, the rest are affected by it.

(Shir Hashirim [Song of Songs] Raba, VI)

Foremost in kingship,
Glorious of right!
To Him say His trusty:
'To Thee, and to Thee,
To Thee, yea to
Thee, To Thee, true, to Thee,
To Thee, Lord, is the sovereignty:
To Him is it becoming,
to Him shall it become!'

All-pure in kingship,
Powerful of right!
To Him say His courtiers:
'To Thee, and to Thee,
To Thee, yea to
Thee, To Thee, true, to Thee,
To Thee, Lord, is the sovereignty:
To Him is it becoming,
to Him shall it become!'

Single in kingship, Mighty of right!
To Him say His wise ones:
'To Thee, and to Thee,
To Thee, yea to
Thee, To Thee, true, to Thee,
To Thee, Lord, is the sovereignty:
To Him is it becoming,
to Him shall it become!'

Exalted in kingship, Revered or
right! To Him say those around Him:
'To Thee, and to Thee, To Thee,
yea to Thee, To Thee, true, to Thee,
To Thee, Lord, is the sovereignty:
To Him is it becoming,
to Him shall it become!'

Gentle in kingship, Redeeming
of right! To Him say His righteous:
'To Thee, and to Thee, To Thee,
yea to Thee, To Thee, true, to Thee,
To Thee, Lord, is the sovereignty:
To Him is it becoming,
to Him shall it become!'

Holy in kingship, Merciful of right!
To Him say His myriads:
'To Thee, and to Thee, To Thee,
yea to Thee, To Thee, true, to Thee,
To Thee, Lord, is the sovereignty:
To Him is it becoming,
to Him shall it become!'

Excellent in kingship, Sustaining
of right! To Him say His perfect:
'To Thee, and to Thee, To Thee,
yea to Thee, To Thee, true, to Thee,
To Thee, Lord, is the sovereignty:
To Him is it becoming,
to Him shall it become!'

דָּגוּל בִּמְלוּכָה, הָדוּר כַּהֲלָכָה, וָתִיקָיו יֹאמְרוּ לוֹ:
לְךָ וּלְךָ, לְךָ כִּי לְךָ, לְךָ אַף לְךָ,
לְךָ יְיָ הַמַּמְלָכָה,
כִּי לוֹ נָאֶה, כִּי לוֹ יָאֶה.

זַכַּאי בִּמְלוּכָה, חָסִין כַּהֲלָכָה, טַפְסְרָיו יֹאמְרוּ לוֹ:
לְךָ וּלְךָ, לְךָ כִּי לְךָ, לְךָ אַף לְךָ,
לְךָ יְיָ הַמַּמְלָכָה,
כִּי לוֹ נָאֶה, כִּי לוֹ יָאֶה.

יָחִיד בִּמְלוּכָה, כַּבִּיר כַּהֲלָכָה, לִמּוּדָיו יֹאמְרוּ לוֹ:
לְךָ וּלְךָ, לְךָ כִּי לְךָ, לְךָ אַף לְךָ,
לְךָ יְיָ הַמַּמְלָכָה,
כִּי לוֹ נָאֶה, כִּי לוֹ יָאֶה.

מוֹשֵׁל בִּמְלוּכָה, נוֹרָא כַּהֲלָכָה, סְבִיבָיו יֹאמְרוּ לוֹ:
לְךָ וּלְךָ, לְךָ כִּי לְךָ, לְךָ אַף לְךָ,
לְךָ יְיָ הַמַּמְלָכָה,
כִּי לוֹ נָאֶה, כִּי לוֹ יָאֶה.

עָנָו בִּמְלוּכָה, פּוֹדֶה כַּהֲלָכָה, צַדִּיקָיו יֹאמְרוּ לוֹ:
לְךָ וּלְךָ, לְךָ כִּי לְךָ, לְךָ אַף לְךָ,
לְךָ יְיָ הַמַּמְלָכָה,
כִּי לוֹ נָאֶה, כִּי לוֹ יָאֶה.

קָדוֹשׁ בִּמְלוּכָה, רַחוּם כַּהֲלָכָה, שִׁנְאַנָּיו יֹאמְרוּ לוֹ:
לְךָ וּלְךָ, לְךָ כִּי לְךָ, לְךָ אַף לְךָ,
לְךָ יְיָ הַמַּמְלָכָה,
כִּי לוֹ נָאֶה, כִּי לוֹ יָאֶה.

תַּקִּיף בִּמְלוּכָה, תּוֹמֵךְ כַּהֲלָכָה, תְּמִימָיו יֹאמְרוּ לוֹ:
לְךָ וּלְךָ, לְךָ כִּי לְךָ, לְךָ אַף לְךָ,
לְךָ יְיָ הַמַּמְלָכָה,
כִּי לוֹ נָאֶה, כִּי לוֹ יָאֶה.

The Land of Israel & the People of Israel

The Holy One, Blessed Be He said to Moses:
The Land of Israel is dear to Me and the People of Israel are dear to Me.
I will take the People of Israel, who are dear to Me, into the Land of Israel, which is dear to Me.

(Bamidbar [Numbers] Raba, XXIII)

The People of Israel — One Nation

As we know, when a man picks up a bundle of stalks together, is he able to break them? But when they are individual stalks, even an infant can break them.
So, you will see that the People of Israel will not be redeemed until they become united.

(Yalkut Shimoni to Nitzavim)

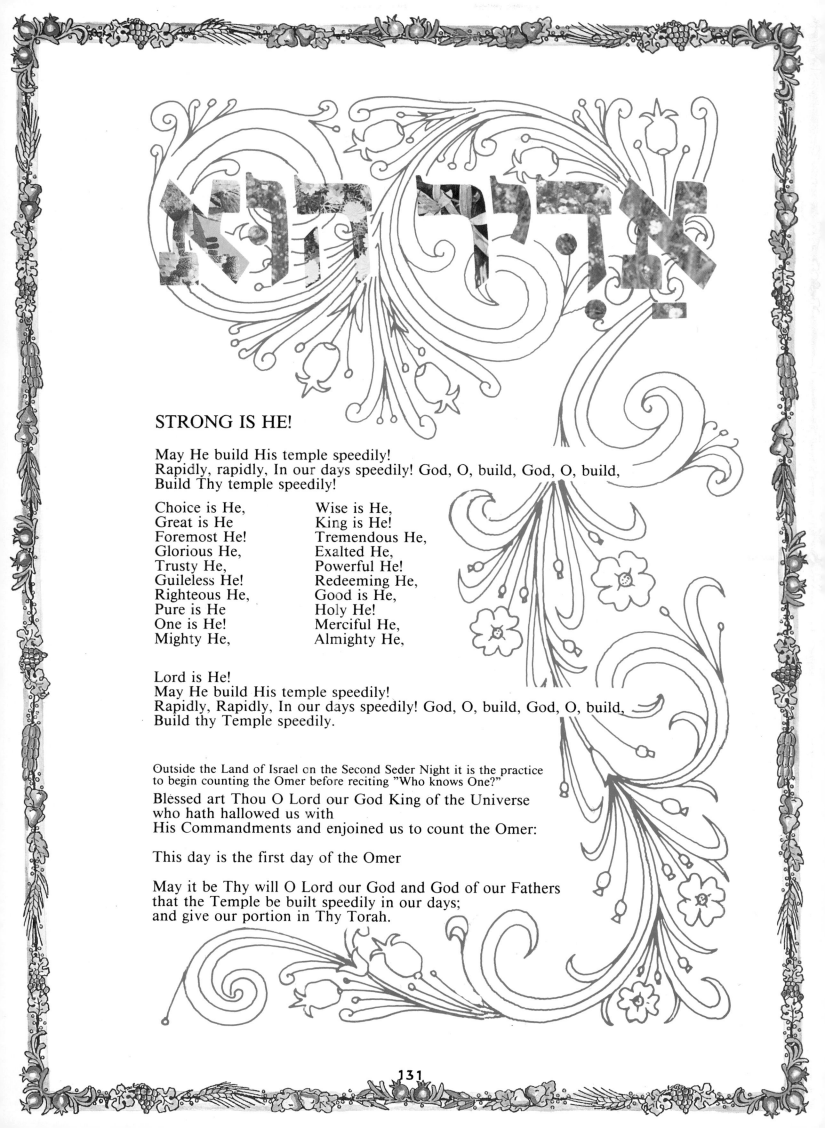

אַדִּיר הוּא

STRONG IS HE!

May He build His temple speedily!
Rapidly, rapidly, In our days speedily! God, O, build, God, O, build,
Build Thy temple speedily!

Choice is He,	Wise is He,
Great is He	King is He!
Foremost He!	Tremendous He,
Glorious He,	Exalted He,
Trusty He,	Powerful He!
Guileless He!	Redeeming He,
Righteous He,	Good is He,
Pure is He	Holy He!
One is He!	Merciful He,
Mighty He,	Almighty He,

Lord is He!
May He build His temple speedily!
Rapidly, Rapidly, In our days speedily! God, O, build, God, O, build,
Build thy Temple speedily.

Outside the Land of Israel on the Second Seder Night it is the practice
to begin counting the Omer before reciting "Who knows One?"

Blessed art Thou O Lord our God King of the Universe
who hath hallowed us with
His Commandments and enjoined us to count the Omer:

This day is the first day of the Omer

May it be Thy will O Lord our God and God of our Fathers
that the Temple be built speedily in our days;
and give our portion in Thy Torah.

The Land of Israel — A Bounteous Land

In the future the Land of Israel will produce cakes and fine garments of silk. As it is written in the Book of Psalms: Let there be an abundance of wheat in the land, on the mountain tops. (Psalms, LXXII, 16).

The sages said: Wheat will grow and reach the height of the palm tree, as high as the mountain tops.
And if you say, it will be difficult to reap it, since it has grown so tall, the text comes to teach us, [the sound of] its fruit will reverberate like the [sound of the leaves in the forests of] Lebanon. (Psalms, LXXII, 16)
The Holy One, Blessed Be He will call forth a wind from His secret places and cause it to blow on the wheat and disperse its seeds.... Then man will go to his field and bring home a handful, from which he will support himself and his household.

(Ketuboth, CXI, B)

אַדִּיר הוּא

יִבְנֶה בֵיתוֹ בְּקָרוֹב,

בִּמְהֵרָה, בִּמְהֵרָה, בְּיָמֵינוּ בְּקָרוֹב,
אֵל בְּנֵה, אֵל בְּנֵה, בְּנֵה בֵיתְךָ בְּקָרוֹב.
בָּחוּר הוּא,
גָּדוֹל הוּא,
דָּגוּל הוּא יִבְנֶה בֵיתוֹ בְּקָרוֹב,
בִּמְהֵרָה, בִּמְהֵרָה, בְּיָמֵינוּ בְּקָרוֹב,
אֵל בְּנֵה, אֵל בְּנֵה, בְּנֵה בֵיתְךָ בְּקָרוֹב.
הָדוּר הוּא,
וָתִיק הוּא,
זַכַּאי הוּא יִבְנֶה בֵיתוֹ בְּקָרוֹב,
בִּמְהֵרָה, בִּמְהֵרָה, בְּיָמֵינוּ בְּקָרוֹב,
אֵל בְּנֵה, אֵל בְּנֵה, בְּנֵה בֵיתְךָ בְּקָרוֹב.
חָסִיד הוּא,
טָהוֹר הוּא,
יָחִיד הוּא יִבְנֶה בֵיתוֹ בְּקָרוֹב,
בִּמְהֵרָה, בִּמְהֵרָה, בְּיָמֵינוּ בְּקָרוֹב,
אֵל בְּנֵה, אֵל בְּנֵה, בְּנֵה בֵיתְךָ בְּקָרוֹב.
כַּבִּיר הוּא,
לָמוּד הוּא,
מֶלֶךְ הוּא יִבְנֶה בֵיתוֹ בְּקָרוֹב,
בִּמְהֵרָה, בִּמְהֵרָה, בְּיָמֵינוּ בְּקָרוֹב,
אֵל בְּנֵה, אֵל בְּנֵה, בְּנֵה בֵיתְךָ בְּקָרוֹב.
נָאוֹר הוּא,
סַגִּיב הוּא,
עִזּוּז הוּא יִבְנֶה בֵיתוֹ בְּקָרוֹב,
בִּמְהֵרָה, בִּמְהֵרָה, בְּיָמֵינוּ בְּקָרוֹב,
אֵל בְּנֵה, אֵל בְּנֵה, בְּנֵה בֵיתְךָ בְּקָרוֹב.
פּוֹדֶה הוּא,
צַדִּיק הוּא,
קָדוֹשׁ הוּא יִבְנֶה בֵיתוֹ בְּקָרוֹב,
בִּמְהֵרָה, בִּמְהֵרָה, בְּיָמֵינוּ בְּקָרוֹב,
אֵל בְּנֵה, אֵל בְּנֵה, בְּנֵה בֵיתְךָ בְּקָרוֹב.
רַחוּם הוּא,
שַׁדַּי הוּא,
תַּקִּיף הוּא יִבְנֶה בֵיתוֹ בְּקָרוֹב,
בִּמְהֵרָה, בִּמְהֵרָה, בְּיָמֵינוּ בְּקָרוֹב,
אֵל בְּנֵה, אֵל בְּנֵה, בְּנֵה בֵיתְךָ בְּקָרוֹב.

The Name of the Lord in the Land of Israel

Rabbi Shimon ben Lakish said in the name of Rabbi Yanai: The Holy One, Blessed Be He lent His great name to the name Israel [in that both names in the Hebrew language share a number of similar letters].

This may be compared to a king who possessed the key to the archives. The king said: If I keep it as it is, it may be lost. Therefore, I will make a chain for it — that if it gets lost, the chain will be evidence of which [key] it is.

So said the Holy One, Blessed Be He: If I leave the People of Israel to be as they now are, they will be swallowed up among the other nations. However, I will lend My great name to them — and they will survive.

(Jerusalem Talmud, Ta'anith LXXXII, Halacha 6)

WHO KNOWS ONE?

Who knows **One**? **One** I know!
One is our God in Heaven and on Earth.

Who knows **Two**? **Two** I know!
Two are the Tables of Covenant:
One is our God in Heaven and on Earth.

Who knows **Three**? **Three** I know!
Three are the Fathers:
Two are the Tables of Covenant:
One is our God in Heaven and on Earth.

Who knows **Four**? **Four** I know!
Four are the Mothers:
Three are the Fathers:
Two are the Tables of Covenant:
One is our God in Heaven and on Earth.

Who knows **Five**? **Five** I know!
Five are the Books of the Torah:
Four are the Mothers:
Three are the Fathers:
Two are the Tables of Covenant:
One is our God in Heaven and on Earth.

אֶחָד מִי יוֹדֵעַ?

אֶחָד

מִי יוֹדֵעַ?
אֶחָד אֲנִי יוֹדֵעַ:
אֶחָד אֱלֹהֵינוּ שֶׁבַּשָּׁמַיִם וּבָאָרֶץ.

שְׁנַיִם

מִי יוֹדֵעַ?
שְׁנַיִם אֲנִי יוֹדֵעַ:
שְׁנֵי לוּחוֹת הַבְּרִית,
אֶחָד אֱלֹהֵינוּ שֶׁבַּשָּׁמַיִם וּבָאָרֶץ.

שְׁלוֹשָׁה

מִי יוֹדֵעַ?
שְׁלוֹשָׁה אֲנִי יוֹדֵעַ:
שְׁלוֹשָׁה אָבוֹת, שְׁנֵי לוּחוֹת הַבְּרִית,
אֶחָד אֱלֹהֵינוּ שֶׁבַּשָּׁמַיִם וּבָאָרֶץ.

אַרְבַּע

מִי יוֹדֵעַ?
אַרְבַּע אֲנִי יוֹדֵעַ:
אַרְבַּע אִמָּהוֹת, שְׁלוֹשָׁה אָבוֹת, שְׁנֵי לוּחוֹת הַבְּרִית,
אֶחָד אֱלֹהֵינוּ שֶׁבַּשָּׁמַיִם וּבָאָרֶץ.

חֲמִשָּׁה

מִי יוֹדֵעַ?
חֲמִשָּׁה אֲנִי יוֹדֵעַ:
חֲמִשָּׁה חֻמְשֵׁי תוֹרָה, אַרְבַּע אִמָּהוֹת,
שְׁלוֹשָׁה אָבוֹת, שְׁנֵי לוּחוֹת הַבְּרִית,
אֶחָד אֱלֹהֵינוּ שֶׁבַּשָּׁמַיִם וּבָאָרֶץ.

The People of Israel are Compared to the Sands

The People of Israel are compared to the sands.
Just as with dust, when you dig a hole in it at evening time, in the morning you find that it has filled up, so all the populace who were missing during the time of King David, were added [to the population] during the time of King Solomon, as it is written: Judah and Israel are as plenteous as the sand on the shores of the sea.

(Psikta D'Rav Kahana, XXXII)

Who knows **Six? Six** I know!
Six are the Orders of the Mishnah:
Five are the Books of the Torah:
Four are the Mothers:
Three are the Fathers:
Two are the Tables of Covenant:
One is our God in Heaven and on Earth.

Who knows **Seven? Seven** I know!
Seven are the days of the Week:
Six are the Orders of the Mishnah:
Five are the Books of the Torah:
Four are the Mothers:
Three are the Fathers:
Two are the Tables of Covenant:
One is our God in Heaven and on Earth.

Who knows **Eight? Eight** I know!
Eight are the days of the Covenant:
Seven are the days of the Week:
Six are the Orders of the Mishnah:
Five are the Books of the Torah:
Four are the Mothers:
Three are the Fathers:
Two are the Tables of Covenant:
One is our God in Heaven and on Earth.

Who knows **Nine? Nine** I know!
Nine are the months of Carrying:
Eight are the days of the Covenant:
Seven are the days of the Week:
Six are the Orders of the Mishnah:
Five are the Books of the Torah:
Four are the Mothers:
Three are the Fathers:
Two are the Tables of Covenant:
One is our God in Heaven and on Earth.

שִׁשָּׁה

מִי יוֹדֵעַ?

שִׁשָּׁה אֲנִי יוֹדֵעַ:

שִׁשָּׁה סִדְרֵי מִשְׁנָה, חֲמִשָּׁה חֻמְשֵׁי תוֹרָה,
אַרְבַּע אִמָּהוֹת,
שְׁלוֹשָׁה אָבוֹת, שְׁנֵי לוּחוֹת הַבְּרִית,
אֶחָד אֱלֹהֵינוּ שֶׁבַּשָּׁמַיִם וּבָאָרֶץ.

שִׁבְעָה

מִי יוֹדֵעַ?

שִׁבְעָה אֲנִי יוֹדֵעַ:

שִׁבְעָה יְמֵי שַׁבְּתָא, שִׁשָּׁה סִדְרֵי מִשְׁנָה,
חֲמִשָּׁה חֻמְשֵׁי תוֹרָה,
אַרְבַּע אִמָּהוֹת, שְׁלוֹשָׁה אָבוֹת, שְׁנֵי לוּחוֹת הַבְּרִית,
אֶחָד אֱלֹהֵינוּ שֶׁבַּשָּׁמַיִם וּבָאָרֶץ.

שְׁמוֹנָה

מִי יוֹדֵעַ?

שְׁמוֹנָה אֲנִי יוֹדֵעַ:

שְׁמוֹנָה יְמֵי מִילָה, שִׁבְעָה יְמֵי שַׁבְּתָא, שִׁשָּׁה סִדְרֵי
מִשְׁנָה, חֲמִשָּׁה חֻמְשֵׁי תוֹרָה, אַרְבַּע אִמָּהוֹת,
שְׁלוֹשָׁה אָבוֹת, שְׁנֵי לוּחוֹת הַבְּרִית,
אֶחָד אֱלֹהֵינוּ שֶׁבַּשָּׁמַיִם וּבָאָרֶץ.

תִּשְׁעָה

מִי יוֹדֵעַ?

תִּשְׁעָה אֲנִי יוֹדֵעַ:

תִּשְׁעָה יַרְחֵי לֵדָה, שְׁמוֹנָה יְמֵי מִילָה, שִׁבְעָה יְמֵי
שַׁבְּתָא, שִׁשָּׁה סִדְרֵי מִשְׁנָה, חֲמִשָּׁה חֻמְשֵׁי תוֹרָה,
אַרְבַּע אִמָּהוֹת, שְׁלוֹשָׁה אָבוֹת, שְׁנֵי לוּחוֹת הַבְּרִית,
אֶחָד אֱלֹהֵינוּ שֶׁבַּשָּׁמַיִם וּבָאָרֶץ.

וְעָמְדוּ רַגְלָיו בַּיּוֹם הַהוּא עַל הַר הַזֵּיתִים

עֲשָׂרָה

מִי יוֹדֵעַ?

עֲשָׂרָה אֲנִי יוֹדֵעַ:

עֲשָׂרָה דִבְּרַיָּא, תִּשְׁעָה יַרְחֵי לֵדָה, שְׁמוֹנָה יְמֵי
מִילָה, שִׁבְעָה יְמֵי שַׁבַּתָּא, שִׁשָּׁה סִדְרֵי מִשְׁנָה,
חֲמִשָּׁה חֻמְשֵׁי תוֹרָה, אַרְבַּע אִמָּהוֹת, שְׁלוֹשָׁה אָבוֹת,
שְׁנֵי לֻחוֹת הַבְּרִית,
אֶחָד אֱלֹהֵינוּ שֶׁבַּשָּׁמַיִם וּבָאָרֶץ.

אַחַד עָשָׂר

מִי יוֹדֵעַ?

אַחַד עָשָׂר אֲנִי יוֹדֵעַ:

אַחַד עָשָׂר כּוֹכְבַיָּא, עֲשָׂרָה דִבְּרַיָּא, תִּשְׁעָה יַרְחֵי
לֵדָה, שְׁמוֹנָה יְמֵי מִילָה, שִׁבְעָה יְמֵי שַׁבַּתָּא, שִׁשָּׁה
סִדְרֵי מִשְׁנָה, חֲמִשָּׁה חֻמְשֵׁי תוֹרָה, אַרְבַּע אִמָּהוֹת,
שְׁלוֹשָׁה אָבוֹת, שְׁנֵי לֻחוֹת הַבְּרִית,
אֶחָד אֱלֹהֵינוּ שֶׁבַּשָּׁמַיִם וּבָאָרֶץ.

שְׁנֵים עָשָׂר

מִי יוֹדֵעַ?

שְׁנֵים עָשָׂר אֲנִי יוֹדֵעַ:

שְׁנֵים עָשָׂר שִׁבְטַיָּא, אַחַד עָשָׂר כּוֹכְבַיָּא, עֲשָׂרָה
דִבְּרַיָּא, תִּשְׁעָה יַרְחֵי לֵדָה, שְׁמוֹנָה יְמֵי מִילָה, שִׁבְעָה
יְמֵי שַׁבַּתָּא, שִׁשָּׁה סִדְרֵי מִשְׁנָה, חֲמִשָּׁה חֻמְשֵׁי תוֹרָה,
אַרְבַּע אִמָּהוֹת, שְׁלוֹשָׁה אָבוֹת, שְׁנֵי לֻחוֹת הַבְּרִית,
אֶחָד אֱלֹהֵינוּ שֶׁבַּשָּׁמַיִם וּבָאָרֶץ.

שְׁלוֹשָׁה עָשָׂר

מִי יוֹדֵעַ?

שְׁלוֹשָׁה עָשָׂר אֲנִי יוֹדֵעַ:

שְׁלוֹשָׁה עָשָׂר מִדַּיָּא, שְׁנֵים עָשָׂר שִׁבְטַיָּא, אַחַד עָשָׂר
כּוֹכְבַיָּא, עֲשָׂרָה דִבְּרַיָּא, תִּשְׁעָה יַרְחֵי לֵדָה, שְׁמוֹנָה
יְמֵי מִילָה, שִׁבְעָה יְמֵי שַׁבַּתָּא, שִׁשָּׁה סִדְרֵי מִשְׁנָה,
חֲמִשָּׁה חֻמְשֵׁי תוֹרָה, אַרְבַּע אִמָּהוֹת, שְׁלוֹשָׁה אָבוֹת,
שְׁנֵי לֻחוֹת הַבְּרִית,

אֶחָד אֱלֹהֵינוּ שֶׁבַּשָּׁמַיִם וּבָאָרֶץ.

Who knows **Ten? Ten** I know!
Ten are the Commandments:
Nine are the months of Carrying:
Eight are the days of the Covenant:
Seven are the days of the Week:
Six are the Orders of the Mishnah:
Five are the Books of the Torah:
Four are the Mothers:
Three are the Fathers:
Two are the Tables of Covenant:
One is our God in Heaven and on Earth.

Who knows **Eleven? Eleven** I know!
Eleven are the Stars:
Ten are the Commandments:
Nine are the months of Carrying:
Eight are the days of the Covenant:
Seven are the days of the Week:
Six are the Orders of the Mishnah:
Five are the Books of the Torah:
Four are the Mothers:
Three are the Fathers:
Two are the Tables of Covenant:
One is our God in Heaven and on Earth.

Who knows **Twelve? Twelve** I know!
Twelve are the Tribes:
Eleven are the Stars:
Ten are the Commandments:
Nine are the months of Carrying:
Eight are the days of the Covenant:
Seven are the days of the Week:
Six are the Orders of the Mishnah:
Five are the Books of the Torah:
Four are the Mothers:
Three are the Fathers:
Two are the Tables of Covenant:
One is our God in Heaven and on Earth.

Who knows **Thirteen? Thirteen** I know!
Thirteen are the Attributes of God:
Twelve are the Tribes:
Eleven are the Stars:
Ten are the Commandments:
Nine are the months of Carrying:
Eight are the days of the Covenant:
Seven are the days of the Week:
Six are the Orders of the Mishnah:
Five are the Books of the Torah:
Four are the Mothers:
Three are the Fathers:
Two are the Tables of Covenant:
One is our God in Heaven and on Earth.

אֶחָד אֱלֹהֵנוּ
שֶׁבַּשָּׁמַיִם
וּבָאָרֶץ

חַד
גַּדְיָא

חַד גַּדְיָא

One only kid, One only kid.

That father bought for two zuzim,
One only kid, One only kid

Then came a cat and ate the kid
That father bought two zuzim,
One only kid, One only kid.

Then came a dog, and bit the cat, that ate the kid
That father bought for two zuzim,
One only kid, One only kid.

Then came a stick, and beat the dog, that bit the cat
That ate the kid
That father bought for two zuzim,
One only kid, One only kid.

Then came the fire, and burned the stick, that beat the dog
That bit the cat, that ate the kid
That father bought for two zuzim,
One only kid, One only kid.

Then water came, and quenched the fire
That burned the stick, that beat the dog
That bit the cat, that ate the kid
That father bought for two zuzim,
One only kid, One only kid.

חַד גַּדְיָא

חַד גַּדְיָא

חַד גַּדְיָא, דְּזַבִּין אַבָּא בִּתְרֵי זוּזֵי, חַד גַּדְיָא, חַד גַּדְיָא.

וְאָתָא שׁוּנְרָא

וְאָכַל לְגַדְיָא, דְּזַבִּין אַבָּא בִּתְרֵי זוּזֵי, חַד גַּדְיָא, חַד גַּדְיָא.

וְאָתָא כַלְבָּא

וְנָשַׁךְ לְשׁוּנְרָא, דְּאָכַל לְגַדְיָא, דְּזַבִּין אַבָּא בִּתְרֵי זוּזֵי, חַד גַּדְיָא, חַד גַּדְיָא.

וְאָתָא חֻטְרָא

וְהִכָּה לְכַלְבָּא, דְּנָשַׁךְ לְשׁוּנְרָא, דְּאָכַל לְגַדְיָא, דְּזַבִּין אַבָּא בִּתְרֵי זוּזֵי, חַד גַּדְיָא, חַד גַּדְיָא.

וְאָתָא נוּרָא

וְשָׂרַף לְחֻטְרָא, דְּהִכָּה לְכַלְבָּא, דְּנָשַׁךְ לְשׁוּנְרָא, דְּאָכַל לְגַדְיָא, דְּזַבִּין אַבָּא בִּתְרֵי זוּזֵי, חַד גַּדְיָא, חַד גַּדְיָא.

וְאָתָא מַיָּא

וְכָבָה לְנוּרָא, דְּשָׂרַף לְחֻטְרָא, דְּהִכָּה לְכַלְבָּא, דְּנָשַׁךְ לְשׁוּנְרָא, דְּאָכַל לְגַדְיָא, דְּזַבִּין אַבָּא בִּתְרֵי זוּזֵי, חַד גַּדְיָא, חַד גַּדְיָא.

Then came an ox, and drank the water
That quenched the fire, that burned the stick,
That beat the dog, that bit the cat, that ate the kid
That father bought for two zuzim,
One only kid, One only kid.

Then came the slaughterer
And slaughtered the ox, that drank the water
That quenched the fire, that burned the stick,
That beat the dog, that bit the cat, that ate the kid
That father bought for two zuzim,
One only kid, One only kid.

Then came the Angel of Death
And slew the slaughterer, that slaughtered the ox
That drank the water, that quenched the fire
That burned the stick, that beat the dog,
That bit the cat, that ate the kid
That father bought for two zuzim,
One only kid, One only kid.

Then came the Holy One, Blessed be He,
And smote the Angel of Death that slew the slaughterer
That slaughtered the ox, that drank the water
That quenched the fire, that burned the stick
That beat the dog, that bit the cat, that ate the kid
That father bought for two zuzim,
One only kid, One only kid.

It is the custom to close the Seder Night by reading the Song of Songs.

וְאָתָא תוֹרָא

וְשָׁתָא לְמַיָּא, דְּכָבָה לְנוּרָא, דְּשָׂרַף לְחֻטְרָא, דְּהִכָּה לְכַלְבָּא, דְּנָשַׁךְ לְשׁוּנְרָא, דְּאָכַל לְגַדְיָא, דְּזַבִּין אַבָּא בִּתְרֵי זוּזֵי, חַד גַּדְיָא, חַד גַּדְיָא:

וְאָתָא הַשּׁוֹחֵט

וְשָׁחַט לְתוֹרָא, דְּשָׁתָא לְמַיָּא, דְּכָבָה לְנוּרָא, דְּשָׂרַף לְחֻטְרָא, דְּהִכָּה לְכַלְבָּא, דְּנָשַׁךְ לְשׁוּנְרָא, דְּאָכַל לְגַדְיָא, דְּזַבִּין אַבָּא בִּתְרֵי זוּזֵי, חַד גַּדְיָא, חַד גַּדְיָא.

וְאָתָא מַלְאַךְ הַמָּוֶת

וְשָׁחַט לְשׁוֹחֵט, דְּשָׁחַט לְתוֹרָא, דְּשָׁתָא לְמַיָּא, דְּכָבָה לְנוּרָא, דְּשָׂרַף לְחֻטְרָא, דְּהִכָּה לְכַלְבָּא, דְּנָשַׁךְ לְשׁוּנְרָא, דְּאָכַל לְגַדְיָא, דְּזַבִּין אַבָּא בִּתְרֵי זוּזֵי, חַד גַּדְיָא, חַד גַּדְיָא.

וְאָתָא הַקָּדוֹשׁ בָּרוּךְ הוּא

וְשָׁחַט לְמַלְאַךְ הַמָּוֶת, דְּשָׁחַט לְשׁוֹחֵט, דְּשָׁחַט לְתוֹרָא, דְּשָׁתָא לְמַיָּא, דְּכָבָה לְנוּרָא, דְּשָׂרַף לְחֻטְרָא, דְּהִכָּה לְכַלְבָּא, דְּנָשַׁךְ לְשׁוּנְרָא, דְּאָכַל לְגַדְיָא, דְּזַבִּין אַבָּא בִּתְרֵי זוּזֵי, חַד גַּדְיָא, חַד גַּדְיָא.

תם ונשלם שבח לאל בורא עולם